TEHRAN TO MALIBU

My Journey in Pursuit of Home

VIOLET BAGHDASARIAN

Copyright © 2021 by Violet Baghdasarian

Tehran to Malibu
Violet Baghdasarian
www.TehranToMalibu.com

All rights reserved. No part of this book may be reproduced or used in any manner without written permission of the publisher except for the use of questions in a book review. For information, address publisher Publish Authority,

First paperback edition April 21, 2021

Cover design lead: Raeghan Rebstock
Editor: Bob Laning

ISBN 978-1-954000-10-0 (paperback)
ISBN 978-1-954000-11-7 (eBook)

Published by Publish Authority
Offices in Newport Beach, CA and Roswell, GA USA
www.PublishAuthority.com

Printed in the United States of America

This book is dedicated to my beautiful family, my husband, and two sons: Michael and Matthew, both of whom I call my M & M's. You give my life purpose and without you two, life would have no meaning. You boys changed my entire perception of life for the better and I couldn't be more appreciative. I love the both of you from the bottom of my heart.

To my sisters and brother, all my nieces and nephews, I love you all very much. Special thanks to my wonderful niece, Bronte. Your birth was the closest thing I had to motherhood at the time and was one of the best things that has ever happened to me. Thank you for your whole-hearted encouragement and continuous support throughout this journey. Without you, this book would not exist. Most importantly, thank you for always undoubtedly believing in me and never letting me forget that I am your role model. I want you to know that although you look up to me, you are far wiser than you think. To my mother, who never ceases to tell her heartfelt stories in such abundance making it impossible to fit all of them in one book. I admire your wisdom and patience and love you so much.

Last but not least, to my late father, Leon Baghdasarian. You left us on Earth sooner than you should have, but I know your spirit has never left my side. I know you found your permanent home up there watching over me and the family like the angel you always were. I will always worship your pure heart which only allowed you to see the good in people. You have touched the hearts of many and left a permanent mark, especially in mine.

Chapter One

MALIBU

Everyone has a story, a story that belongs to you and you only. Those events that we experience, which turn into our stories, are compiled together in our memories and make us who we are. They influence who we want to be or what the world is allowing us to endure. I found passion for reading from my preteen age years, and there was a reason why one of my favorite hobbies was reading. I loved reading books because I envisioned myself as the main character in every story that I read—in a way, being a part of someone else's story instead of my own. Most of the time, I pretended to be either a princess living in my imaginary castle or a mother who was an Armenian genocide survivor, having to care for her children. My two dolls were my pretend children in this scenario.

I felt so connected to these fictional characters that I

actually started to feel their emotions and pain. At one point, I even started to cough up blood, just like the character in my book. This weird occurrence—of me coughing up blood—took me to many doctors' offices, but no one could determine what the cause was. I lived inside my books and pictured myself in every situation partly because I was still on the journey of figuring out who I was in my own reality. I was a little too curious for a little girl and wanted to try new things and experience things out of the norm to find where I stood in the world.

Not surprisingly, after the girl in my book died, my illness disappeared. I came to realize that maybe my condition was a result of a figment of my imagination. I slowly realized that my mind wasn't just trying to mimic the character's emotions, but her physical illnesses too. This is where I learned that our mind is much more potent than I had previously given credit. It's fascinating how our psyche can manipulate even our physical sensations. I believed this was my mind's coping mechanism for my complete mental dedication to a story that was not mine.

The act of purchasing a book gave me the same amount of happiness as reading it. My home library was expanding, and so was my popularity among my friends. They borrowed books from me rather than the library since they found it more convenient. We had similar interests considering we had things in common, so they trusted my taste in literature. I used to and still do, love the smell of books, both old and freshly printed. They each have a unique scent, yet they provoke the same feeling of bliss. I had a six-foot-tall metal bookshelf with five shelves overloaded with storybooks. It was in the middle of the staircase with a window above it, and it was my favorite place to be.

Our house had a vast terrace even more spacious than the living room and family room combined. The terrace was covered with grape vines wrapped in every direction, maintained by my mother. She did a great job taking care of them and pruning the grapes, and it was a beautiful addition to our terrace. We enjoyed watching them grow and eventually ripen enough to be indulged in all summer long. Most summer nights, we slept on mattresses on the terrace where the grapevines were. The sky was so clear, making it magical to see so many shooting stars in the sky upon which we could wish.

Our mornings began with the sight of an abundance of green grapes thriving all around us. They looked so appetizing that we would give in and grab handfuls of them to eat for breakfast. I can still vividly remember the luscious, juicy flavor of these big, crisp grapes, the best I have probably ever eaten in my life. The grapes weren't the only delicious thing about the vines. We used the leaves for making a dish called dolma. This was a typical meal in Mediterranean cuisine and the surrounding region in the Middle East. The stuffing for dolma was meat, rice, oil, and tomato paste, with various herbs and spices. The meat-free and vegan version of this was called sarma, which was the same recipe, except without the meat. Sarma or meat dolmas are generally served warm.

This wasn't a quick and easy meal to make, as it took several hours to wrap the grape leaves with the stuffing. A lot of time and effort goes into carefully preparing this meal. We all enjoyed the delicious dolmas that my mother would make with love. My mother still makes her delicious dolmas from the grape leaves that I grow in my backyard. My children and I still get to enjoy her homemade dolmas that remain unmatched. It was a traditional get together meal for Armenians because nobody would turn down a meticulously delicious, prepared dolma.

If I could revisit any place on Earth one more time before the end of my lifetime, it would be the place where I have experienced my most everlasting memories: my home. It is where I created beautiful memories with my friends, family, and even the fictional characters whose stories became a part of mine, as they helped me develop my own. It is the place that gave me the sweetest tasting grapes first thing in the morning. The place where I would sleep on the rooftop in the summer with my siblings in the fresh, cool breeze. The city that I remember had clean air and acknowledged all four seasons accordingly. Unfortunately, this was a reality that is now a distant memory. Tehran today has very potent pollution levels leaving the skies grayer than before. I've even heard that on days with high pollution levels, elders, and people with compromised respiratory systems are advised to stay indoors.

Being a young Armenian girl passionate about my heritage, I always wondered how and what drove so many Armenians to migrate to Iran. I was curious why my ancestors moved from their homeland centuries ago, even before the Armenian genocide, to a place that was predominantly Islamic. From the time of my birth, through my preteen life, the country was ruled by the Shah, who pushed the country to adopt Western-oriented secular modernization. Under the Shah's rule, some degree of cultural freedom was allowed. Iran's economic and educational opportunities had expanded, with Britain and the U.S. considering Iran as their principal ally in the Middle East. Due to Iran's large supply of oil and its shared border with the Soviet Union, Britain and the U.S. fully backed the Iranian government. Communists and religious members of society disliked the Shah and his pro-western government.

Eventually, the dismissal of a multiparty rule set the stage for the infamous Revolution. While growing up, I became confused about how and why my Armenian ancestors ended up in a place with such limitations as Iran. Armenians are Christians belonging to the Apostolic church, one of the oldest Christian churches. They were among the first people to adopt Christianity. Many explanations and theories were shared, but it was not until later that I learned something that put the puzzle pieces together. It was before the third century A.D. when Iran had more influence on Armenian culture than any of its other neighbors. The two different cultures shared many religious, political, and linguistic elements and traditions, and at one time, even shared the same dynasty.

However, Sasanian policies and the Armenian conversion to Christianity in the fourth century alienated the Armenians from Zoroastrian Iran and oriented them toward the West. The Arab conquests, which ended the Iranian Empire and converted Iran to Islam in the seventh century, culturally separated the Armenians even further from their neighbors. In the eleventh century, the Seljuk Turks drove thousands of Armenians to Iran and Azerbaijan. They worked as artisans and merchants in these countries. The Mongol conquest of Iran in the thirteenth century enabled the Armenians. They were treated favorably by the victors to play a significant role in the international trade among the Caspian, Black, and Mediterranean Seas. Armenian merchants and artisans settled in the Iranian cities bordering historical Armenia.

I am a descendant amongst many of the Armenians born and raised in Tehran, the capital of Iran. In my family and most other Armenian families living in a country other than their motherland, we identified as Armenian first, then as Christian. It is unfortunate to say that I have no memories of going to church regularly other than on Christian holidays. It was hard for Armenian families to attend church services, as Saturday and Sunday were considered workdays, and schools were in session on those days. Although this was a problematic constraint I experienced from growing up in a non-Christian country, I still wouldn't trade my hometown and memories for anything else because all of my experiences there have contributed to the creation of my own story.

Despite living in Iran for hundreds of years, Armenians always maintained their identity as Armenian people. This, despite almost being eliminated from the face of the earth. When you are Armenian, you are also familiar with the devastating Genocide of 1915, known as the Armenian Genocide. During the downfall of the Ottoman Empire, the Ottoman Turks systematically organized and exercised the massacre of about 1.5 million innocent Armenian people residing in Constantinople, which is present-day Istanbul. Amongst these Armenians, many of them were highly intelligent public figures and aristocrats. Our people were slaughtered in front of their families. The most barbaric of them all was the killing of premature babies, pried out of a soon to be mother's womb and killed right in front of their mother. The mother and the rest of the family were murdered afterward. Our most valuable literature, beautiful homes and, and, most importantly, innocent lives perished.

Some Armenians' lives were spared for the moment, only to be brutally murdered later when mothers and children were forced to walk towards the Syrian desert. Thousands of Armenians were ordered to exit Turkey, while many were killed before they could make it out.

Expectant mothers walked for countless days and nights, deprived of food and water. They walked barefoot, some even carrying their young toddlers on their backs in hopes of seeking shelter. These are amongst the people who carried on the Armenian gene for decades to come, giving them the title of survivors of the Armenian Genocide.

Armenians worldwide have an annual, widespread, and peaceful protest, occurring every April 24th, memorializing the Armenian Genocide. This protest is held not only as an act of remembrance but as a plea for Turkey and other nations to acknowledge the Armenian Genocide for being what it was; a genocide. Countries today, especially Turkey, have failed to recognize the Armenian Genocide through their active denial. April 24 is the chosen day for this because it has been established that on this day, the most crucial and abundant murders of influential Armenian leaders and intellectuals took place. These protests occurred back home in Iran as well, and members of the Armenian clubs all around were proud participants. As an Armenian club member myself, it was our responsibility to make banners during the days leading up to the protest.

There is no Armenian family in the world that doesn't know of a survivor, or hasn't heard of an Armenian Genocide survivor's story, or that is unaware of the genocide. I came across two people in my life who have shaped my understanding of the genocide. The first was my choir teacher. Mr. Martick was otherwise known as, in Armenian, Paron Martick. He was an older man in his sixties at the time, who always spoke passionately about Armenians and our culture. He talked a lot about his personal connection to the genocide, and it made us feel connected as well.

He and his mother faced the ultimate loss a family could have when he and his mother lost the rest of their family to the bloodshed of the Genocide. I do not remember ever seeing him laugh. He was very stern and severe with a consistently sad demeanor. He had a challenging burden to carry, so everyone, including myself, always excused his sadness. Every time we sang Armenian cultural or national songs, I could see his teary eyes seeking a place to be unseen. Not even the funniest of jokes would make a chuckle slip from his mouth.

The other genocide story I heard was from an Armenian woman named Tikin Sceeran, whom I met at the Armenian club where we participated in the protests. Tikin is Armenian for Mrs. I only knew her for a short time, but her stories and advice remain as everlasting memories in my heart. I can still remember Tikin Sceeran from the club vividly, from her face down to her hairstyle. At the club late at night, when we were getting ready to commemorate the Armenian Genocide by putting banners together and highlighting mottos for the big day, all while listening to sorrowful stories, I found out about Tikin Screeran's maddening truth. She was an Armenian genocide survivor. She was a descendant of the Armenian Genocide itself. Her family and relatives were ordered to leave town to spare their lives. She was a little girl then, but she managed to vividly remember how they were sent through a desert on foot caravan, as men were being killed left and right. Her grandfather and the elderly were shot for slowing down the traffic. Young boys were shoved off the cliffs into the river. Little kids died of starvation and diseases, which went uncured. Her family and relatives died one after another before her fragile and exhausted eyes. She talked passionately about her horrible survival story. Her younger brother and mother survived, and she believes God must have been watching over her little sister, who was in her mother's womb. They ended up in the path of the rescue mission people who were in search of Armenian Victims. Anger was going through my entire body and was cursing every hand that had the blood of innocent Armenians. Hearing Tikin Sceeran's story made me wish an eternity of Hell for all those who had the blood of my Armenian people resting on their hands.

The Ottoman Empire's systematic deportation and killing of 1.5 million Armenians shortly after World War I is still denied by Turkey today. The Turkish government denies the concept of a systematic plan for wiping out the Armenian people. Some survivors of the genocide lost contact with their family members and were scattered to various regions of the Middle East, Russia, and Europe. A few migrated to the American and Australian continents as well. Most Armenian survivors fled the Ottoman Empire in search of refuge. The survivors who managed to escape carried their Armenian heritage and memories proudly. They preserved the Armenian language and cultural traditions in their new countries, ensuring that nothing could eliminate the Armenian people.

Chapter Two

MY DAD I

When I think about how I got to this point in my life, starting in Tehran, Iran, the first thing that comes to my mind is rule-breaking; rules and regulations that were in the form of abiding by the standards of normalcy. As it is evident in my story, my life's path has not been linear. There was also an ecstatic nature about my unique experiences that is deserving to be heard. I believe in destiny, but I also maintain the belief that our own actions have the power to control many aspects of our lives. In the least narcissistic way, I do consider myself rather unique. I owe it all to the powerful force inside of me that is driving me to something at all times for an unknown reason. A force that allows me to make my decisions in a way that ends up being favorable or protecting even if that decision isn't a common one.

Yes, I believe a strong, powerful force protects me and

guides me as I navigate through my life, not knowing what the future may hold. Is it because of my religious beliefs? Is it because of my inner intuition? Is it because it was leading me to write this book? I don't know if I will ever find out the answer to that, and that is okay. I know that whatever is protecting me will continue watching over me until I reach my life's destiny. Therefore, I am saying I have gone through pain or struggle like everyone else because that is inevitable. Nobody on Earth has a perfect experience, and mine was furthest from perfection. This force that protected me and allowed me to walk away from life's most challenging hardships placed me back on my path with more strength than I had initially. I have always managed to persevere and walk away with resilience, and I have something to thank for that.

Sometimes in life, we cannot obtain answers to specific questions even if we were the ones who asked them, but as my mother always said, "Don't be afraid of uncertainty, my child. There has been a guardian angel protecting you since your conception." My mother was right. Sometimes the unknown is better left a mystery. The importance was that I knew deep down; we all had some type of influence that wrote our destiny. She told me the story of how she thought about having an abortion after finding out she was pregnant with me. She thought it was too selfish to add another life to the chaotic and messy situation that constituted her life. My parents had so much on their plate after my father's sickness and uprising disputes with our extended family that a child was a distant reality.

Initially, she decided to have an abortion, which instigated an uncharted territory of conversation between her and my father. My father always wanted to have more children and had a specific wish to have six, but supported her decision without a doubt and did not try to dissuade her since the timing for expanding their family wasn't ideal for either of them. Abortion was legal and so common in Iran at the time that the government would regularly advertise the notion on TV that the fewer children you have, the more comfortable your life will be. Ironically, abortion was always against my mother's belief system, and it was never an option. She would get distraught, hearing about a relative or a friend who was undergoing an abortion, as she saw this as an easy fix to a complicated situation.

Until this very day, the thought of when she sat in that abortion clinic waiting to hear her name gives her chills. After weighing their options, my parents found themselves at an abortion clinic, determined to go ahead with the procedure because they felt this was their only option. As my mother was sitting in that cold, unwelcoming metal chair in the waiting room with my father's hand resting in her lap, she saw something from the corner of her eye. A pale, colorless woman with a sorrowful expression on her face walked past them catching my mother's attention. The sight of that woman made my mother sick to her stomach because she knew the reason for her sadness. She couldn't even look in her direction, knowing that she was going to be feeling that same sadness in just a few minutes. Without saying a word, my parents got up and left the clinic. She always reminded me that I am not only a gift from above, but I am a miracle. She attributes my life today to God's grace for giving her the urge to walk out of that office. If she didn't make that decision, well, I wouldn't be here right now.

When my mother entered her second trimester, my father suggested giving up their baby (me) to his younger brother, who was desperate to adopt me. He had found out about my parents wanting to end the pregnancy, so he offered and even pleaded to adopt the child. He was married for eight years, and his wife could not bear a child. His brother knew they could never have a biological child and did not care what the sex of the baby was. Of course, they preferred a baby as close to their bloodline as possible, so this was their perfect opportunity. He assured my dad that he would make an exceptional father and asked him to allow him to be one.

The innocent talk of adoption slowly turned into a real option and gave my parents an alternative for their unborn child. This option of giving me up for adoption by my aunt and uncle was considered the best compared to keeping me for several factors. The main one being that my parents just weren't at a time in their lives to be able to commit emotionally to a newborn baby. The other was that my uncle and aunt were desperate to have a child. My parents kept thinking that I could potentially have a better life with them. Although this was contemplated, my mother could never gather up enough heart to commit to the plan leaving my aunt and uncle short from a definite yes.

It was the night of March 20th when my mother was rushed to the hospital to give birth to me. The Persian people in Tehran and all over Iran were ready to celebrate Nowruz, otherwise known as Iranian New Year. This holiday was not something taken lightly. It was the most celebrated and eventful holiday of the year. Families were getting together, neighbors were visiting each other from door to door and exchanging food, and friends were throwing parties and wishing each other wellness and happiness in the new year to come. Nowruz is no small celebration. It is like New Year and Thanksgiving all at once, including various delicious meals, rice with spices, pastries, all sorts of sweets, gatherings. People were so thrilled and excited about the new year that the streets were filled with dancing and exchanging gifts.

Nowruz is the celebration of Persian New Year, but the festival was not limited to the Persian people. Nowruz means new day. It is no coincidence that it falls on the first day of Spring, and I also believe that it was no coincidence that a new life - mine, was born that day. The Iranian calendar is solar, meaning that time is determined through astronomical observations of the earth's movement around the sun. So, the first day of the year always kicks off with the natural phenomenon of the vernal equinox. It is not a religious holiday, but instead can be seen as a universal celebration of new beginnings. It is a time for wishing prosperity in the upcoming chapter of our lives and welcoming the future to close the chapter on the past. Schools and businesses are also closed for two weeks, giving Iranians time off to spend the beginning of their new chapter with their families. Nowruz influenced families to use the time for initiating new life goals and, most importantly, as an excuse to change their entire wardrobes. Just like every other holiday, Nowruz follows its own traditions. Among these traditions was the "Haft Sin" table, which is set with seven symbolic items, starting with the Farsi letter "S." They include wheatgrass, herbs, and dried fruits. These were all representations of various prosperity metaphors for the New Year, including health, wealth, and prosperity. For example, "sir," the word for garlic, represents protection from illness and evil, while "serkeh," vinegar, represents longevity and patience. Mirrors, candles, decorated eggs, water, and various fruits are also on the tables.

Many families also place a goldfish in a bowl on the table for good luck and poetry books to symbolize education and enlightenment. My mother still recalls the hospital's Haft Sin table and the state of merriment on the day that I was born like it was yesterday. Nowruz holidays usually start a few days before the new year and extend until the 13th of the new year. This happy and celebratory state of the country was an extra unique addition to my mother giving birth to me. She was celebrating the birth of her new child and being uplifted by the promises of the New Year. Since I was only a newborn and can't recall anything even if I tried, I can only imagine how festive it was.

A few painful hours passed since my mother had arrived at the hospital, and she was going through immense pain, trying to give birth to an eight-and-a-half-pound baby. One of the nurses offered a paid-for epidural shot, thanks to a family that had preordered it but hadn't used it. Back in the day, pregnant women were required to order that shot in advance of their delivery time through their OBGYN. If you didn't preorder a shot before going into labor, then as unfortunate as it sounds, you weren't going to get one. My mother didn't think she would need it, so she did not order one and was at a painful realization that she was mistaken.

A nurse told my mother that an injection had been ordered and was ready for a relative of a member of Iran's royal family. They were admitted to the same hospital as my mother at the same time. One could look at this as a New Year's gift to my mother and as a sign of good fortune for the upcoming year. Considering I was a noticeably large baby, the gift turned into the best New Year's present she could have received. Decades later, this lucky gift changed my mother's outlook on pregnancies, which resulted in her advising me in favor of using one, especially during my first pregnancy.

The New Year and the celebration of my birth became intertwined as one, the moment the hospital staff simultaneously shouted, "Happy New Year!". The nurse placed me in my mother's arms in the middle of the happily shouting voices and congratulated her on her new baby girl and gently said, "Happy New Year to you!" Overflowing with omens of good luck during every part of the night, my mother looked at me and immediately knew that nobody could take her baby away. She knew that she could never give me up because of how much love she felt for me in such a short time. Despite their potential adoption plans, my mother knew it was no longer an option for her as soon as her soul interlocked with mine the moment we met.

My aunt from my mother's side picked the name Violet, and Violet, my name became. I was a Nowruz baby (New Year baby), which also made me a Spring baby. After experiencing so many emotions and surprises regarding her pregnancy until my birth, my mom called me her good luck baby. Many decisions were made that resulted in the life I lived, and it started with my mother deciding to keep her baby daughter. The way I see this now is that my mother had options regarding her baby, but yet something magical and indescribable made her make the decision that she did in the hospital the moment she held me. She always said I was born into this world to love and be loved.

It wasn't until several years after my father's death that I figured out why he decided to leave Iran and start a new life in another country. His heart was broken by his brother, who most painfully deceived him. His unfaithful brother was not only immediate family, but he was his business partner. He took advantage of my father's most valued moral principle of honesty by his deception when he cheated him out of his share of the business (the details of which will be discussed later). My father felt so disappointed and defeated by this level of betrayal by one of his siblings, the one whom he trusted and confided in the most. Spending long hours and weeks working away from his home, he trusted his brother with his money, properties, other financial holdings, and his life.

The betrayal of my father occurred sometime between 1960 and 1963, before I was even born. This time period also marked a turning point in the lives of many Iranians and my parents. It was during the reign of Mohamad Reza Shah Pahlavi and the time of the uprising of the national development program, called "The White Revolution." It included construction to expand roads, railroads, and air networks. Industrial expansion was promoted by the Pahlavi regime, while political parties that resisted the Shah's absolute consolidation of power were silenced and pushed into the margins. In 1961, when the Shah dissolved the 20th Majlis (the national legislative body of Iran), clearing the way for his new plan: The Land Reform Law of 1962.

Many wealthy individuals in Iran possessed large bodies of land used for agriculture and harvesting. Under this new law, the feudal system was abolished, resulting in the purchase of land from those individuals and redistributing them to smaller agricultural workers. However, landowners were compensated for their losses and were offered shares of state-owned Iranian industries. There was no official land registry yet; instead, the land ownership for the redistributed land was transferred through title deeds. This was how the documents represented a specific measured area of land.

Because this new law was brand new and the country had no experience with this new socio-economic concept, it resulted in some difficulties. Title deeds transferred the land, which created an opportunity for greedy people to gain ownership titles fraudulently. They did this by having the government wrongfully issue them ownership to land that did not belong to them. The troublesome uprisings of this new reform law did not affect my father's business, but the lack of an official land registry did. This shortcoming, the lack of security, allowed my uncle to easily alter their business and property agreement by entitling himself to a much larger share. The business that was established and built from scratch by two brothers and the properties that were owned equally by the both of them were now primarily owned by my uncle, leaving my father with an unfair smaller portion.

Due to the influx of construction in Iran, many new projects needed completion. This is how my father played a role in all of this. He was a private contractor and a very hardworking and successful one. Most of his work was on the roads, dams, and bridges, resulting in his work being predominantly in other cities. He could only come to visit two or three times a month and only stay for a few days. Due to all of the new construction, there was such high demand in his field, resulting in him working long sleepless hours. He was very stressed and under a great deal of pressure. As demands increased, he would work increasingly harder to meet them. According to my mother, his job wasn't the only stressor in his life.

Things were becoming suspicious regarding the family business, in the sense that my mother was having thoughts of uneasiness regarding our uncle's involvement with our finances. She felt like she was losing control over her finances and was feeling a sense of financial hardship coming their way. While my father was away busy with a heavier workload, my mother was skeptical about her brother-in-law's involvement in the business. She noticed his distancing from the family and had a gut feeling that he was doing something behind their back. Although I was not born yet, my mother was taking care of my three siblings—two toddlers and one infant. Having to take care of all her children, she didn't have much time to intervene.

Despite her reluctance to act upon her assumptions, she knew she could not just abandon her inclination. As she was waiting for my father to come home from his long-distance job project so she could discuss the situation, the situation itself was becoming grave. She did not know the precise cause of their financial distress, but she was noticing a change. She was not getting the right amount of money my father was sending her through his brother. The money flow in the bank accounts to which my mother had access did not correspond with the deposits to which my father was keeping track. All of this validated my mother's initial assumption that my uncle was the cause of their problems.

My father was away from his family, working hard and sending his honest earnings to his family through a joint business account shared with my mother. The only other person who had access to this account was his brother. He was supposed to take care of the business expenses and manage the properties they owned together while my father was out of town. But sure enough, he took hold of that account as his own and started making false claims about the portion of the money to which he was entitled.

My mother knew she couldn't wait any longer for my father to get home, so one day she decided to call him and tell him her concerns about his brother. My father, always seeing the good in people, found it hard to believe that his own brother would be taking advantage of him and his family like that. In response, my father accused my mother of misinterpreting the things that she saw as suspicious enough to be warning signs. He trusted his brothers, and it was hard for him to believe that the one closest to him was committing fraud against him and putting his family at the brink of financial risk as collateral. Harm had already run its course by the time my father returned to Tehran. There was indeed fraud occurring in the family business, which was confirmed when my father returned. Large sums of money were lost, properties sold, and financial records gone with the wind.

Even up until this day, I still cannot believe why my father failed to seek legal action. Perhaps he did not want to have his blood brother arrested, or maybe it was a lack of evidence, or perhaps it was simply how destiny ran its course. The way my father was cheated by the person closest to him hurt more than any tremendous tangible loss, such as his money and estates. According to my mother, he did not want to accept the reality of what happened and had a hard time trying. For being the loving and selfless man he was, he suffered more than he deserved.

A few days after my father was welcomed home from his long work trip to dishonesty and financial hardship, he had a stroke. I still attribute this to the extreme emotional distress he suffered through the betrayal of his brother. My older sister remembers that night, and she says that when our father came home from work, he was arguing with our mother at the dinner table. She noticed something weird about his face during dinner. It was moving slowly toward one side, and he started talking strangely. Father's deformed face, as it was preparing itself for a terrible event, was a horrifying sight. He was rushed to the hospital, where he remained for a few months. During that time, my mother promised never to bring up what happened between my father and uncle. She took this promise lightly, and even after his death, she never stopped talking about it, not even to this day.

After my father recovered from his stroke, my mother accompanied him on several occasions when he went on his business trips until I was born. Traveling would have been too difficult with four little kids. That is when my father decided to move out of the country and start a new life elsewhere, hopefully, to the United States. Some of the most vivid memories that I have of my father were when he returned from his job missions. Soon after, my father was back on the road and off to work. During the time he would visit, time would fly by, and as a little girl who loved spending time with her dad, the time I had with him was never enough.

I loved having my dad around so much, but the time would end, and he had to leave us again. I savored every minute I had with my dad while I could because I knew that it was temporary, and he had to leave for work again. We would spend hours talking together and playing games. My father was masculine, yet he always had a soft spot for his little girl; me. Not only did all of us miss seeing him because we only saw him a few weeks at a time, but we were not able to hear his voice either. Having a telephone at home was not a part of the norm back then. We were not the only family without a phone. Very rarely, someone would have a telephone at their home. "Back in the day," when I was a child, phone numbers had to be ordered, and it would take anywhere up to five or ten years to get assigned one.

We had to communicate with our father somehow, so the only way was through letters. Sometimes he would come back before he received the letters we sent him, and it was even better because we could share everything we had to say to him directly. He usually arrived in the late evening or at night when we were asleep. My mother didn't want him to wake us up, so we didn't find out until the next morning that he had arrived. I still think it was also because she missed him and didn't want to share him with us and enjoyed a few hours alone with him. My father missed us so much, and his excitement would take over and wake us up anyway. I always sensed a trace of disappointment on my mother's face when he would wake us up to greet us. She always said that when he interrupted our sleep just to greet us, he behaved worse than a little kid told not to eat the candy that's right in front of him. She would say, "They have school tomorrow," or, "They just went to bed," The excuses to stop him from waking us up were endless. My mother was much stricter than my father, especially with anything involving our school schedule.

Unlike my mother, I can't remember a single time my father got mad at anyone. He was very gentle and soft-spoken despite his physical build. He was tall and masculine, and according to my mother, he was very handsome. She must have been very attracted to him because, according to her, she had many suitors to choose from, but my father was always the one. Despite her variety of men to choose from, she seemed to find romance only in my father's eyes, who was twenty years older than her.

She married my father when she was only twenty years old, but their love was created in the stars.

I loved waking up in the mornings to see his face knowing he was home for the next few weeks. He had a unique way of waking me up, and that was tickling my feet with a feather. Every time I felt a soft material touch my feet awakening me from my sleep, I would know that only meant one thing; my dad was home. One thing with my father was that he never came home empty-handed from his trips. After greeting him, I would run to his suitcase for candy or toys.

I wasn't the only one who would get overly excited for his return and souvenirs. A medley of people, including friends, relatives, and neighbors, would come to our house for his famous gifts from his travels abroad; some we would never see at other times except upon my father's visits home. Other than our candy and toys, the things he would often bring back were whiskey, Winston cigarettes, and perfumes. Iranian people had a distinct fascination with American products, all of which were always in my father's luggage, ready to be gifted to those around him.

My father was the most selfless man that I knew, which is why it is such a great disappointment to grow up later to find out that he was treated so poorly. He would put his loved ones before him, and he treated strangers with the same benevolence. My father would always go out of his way for everyone regardless of their relation to him. My mother always tells me that my need to give rather than to receive is a characteristic inherited by my father. Through all of my father's surprise visits and the beautiful memories we shared together, I learned a lot from him and the limited time we shared. I learned how to miss, but most importantly, how to love.

Chapter Three

MY DAD II

Life is fragile, and I learned this in the most challenging way possible to man. I have discovered in many various events in my life how easy it is to lose everything in such a short moment in time. A loss so significant that it can alter the way you look at everything you previously took for granted. I was only ten years old when I saw the fragility that lies within human life. I was traumatized by an unpredictable childhood experience that drastically changed my life forever in one day. No one trained me for something like this; a child's worst nightmare. How could anyone prepare a little girl to witness her father passing away. My father's unexpected and untimely death shattered my happy and innocent world. It broke my heart into a million pieces that could never mend together again. Losing a parent is every child's nightmare, but my nightmare came true. It felt like a tornado plowed through our house and tore off the roof of our beautiful home. Our father was the roof keeping our family together, and without him, we lost our sense of home.

It was a chilly, drizzly spring afternoon when my school bus dropped me off at home. It caught me off guard when my mother wasn't waiting to greet me. We lived in a three-story house, and someone was renting the first floor. Our tenant let me in the door but didn't say a single word to greet me. I ran upstairs and what immediately came to my attention was the trail of blood on the rug and stairs. It was such a deep red; it almost looked brown, fooling me into thinking that someone had spilled coffee. That seemed logical, especially when I saw a bowl full of that dark substance in the kitchen sink. I had never seen my house that messy before. My mother was and still is a very tidy woman to such an extent that she can't sit at the breakfast table if the house isn't clean to her liking.

From what I remember, the house looked and felt very strange, and it wasn't just the mess. I sat down to do my homework and heard my sisters walking through the front door one after another from school. By the evening, my aunt showed up. She told us that my father was not feeling well and that my mother would stay with him in the hospital that night. He did not look sick to me that morning, nor did he seem sick the night prior. Looking back at my childhood days, I had never seen my father ill. I always knew him for the healthy and strong man he was. What could have possibly happened to him within the few hours I was gone for school? My older sister later told me that the dark substance I saw all over our house and in the bowl was my father's blood, not coffee.

If I had known that morning was going to be the last moment I had with my father, I would have told him how much I loved him and would have hugged him before leaving for school. Did he think about me before his death? Did he think about how lost I would be without him in this big scary world? I was not allowed to visit him in the hospital, no matter how hard I tried. Everyone was dishonest with me and tried to convince me that my father was getting better and would come home to us very soon. Well, he never did, and he ended up passing away at the hospital. I found out about his death when my mother came home after spending two full days and nights at the hospital wailing. I knew he was gone before the words came out of her mouth. In just a few hours, people rushed to our house wearing black from head to toe in their specially reserved mourning attire, as if it was a competition.

No one was talking to or paying any attention to me. It was as if I didn't exist, and I suddenly felt invisible. I guess no one knew how to handle the situation we were in and didn't know what to say. I think a part of it was that nobody could build up enough courage to face me. I had so many questions arising in my confused young girl's head. Did I do something wrong? Why is no one paying any attention to me? What really happened to my father? Why did he die? I still, to this day, don't have a definite answer to any of those questions. The main mystery being that last question, why did he die?. There are many different versions of the cause of his death among us, his children. We told others that he had a stroke. There is some truth to that response because he did have a stroke about eleven years before his death. The cause of his death remains a mystery to his family and especially me. Sometimes my siblings and I talk about our father's death and the events leading up to it, and we always fail to reach a consensus. Even my mother sometimes changes her story or tries to avoid talking about his death at all.

I know that she knows a lot more about the story than she has been sharing with us. Perhaps this is her method of sparing us any more heartache. The doctors must have shared information about the autopsy with our mother at the hospital, which wasn't communicated to us. Is she going to take this secret with her to her grave? Did she even have all of the answers to this mystery? Was his death a suicide? Was his death an effect of his stroke that he had many years ago? Was he murdered in cold blood? If there was someone with my father's blood on his hands, why was there no investigation after his death? Instead, hundreds of relatives and friends flooded our house and camped out for forty days to mourn. This old Armenian tradition consists of friends and relatives grieving with the family suffering a loss, for a full forty days.

Listening to the voices of people talking about my

father, like they knew him better than I, wasn't an easy noise to cancel out. I kept hearing them say things like, "he seemed healthy both physically and mentally," or, "he had started from scratch and built a new life," or, "he sent his son abroad just a few months ago, and they were going to join him very soon, what a waste." "What could have gone wrong?" I heard these painfully accurate statements from the conversations in my house, against my own will. As if I was invisible, and my presence did not matter at all. If I was noticed at all, it was when a guest needed tending to or some service provided. They would order me around and ask me to serve them something to eat or drink. They would usually ask for Halvah (confectionery dessert). The traditional Armenian recipe consists of flour, sugar, and butter. If the request wasn't for this sweet delicacy, it was for something not so sweet, such as cigarettes, lighters, or an ashtray.

I still cannot comprehend the reason or need behind the abundant smoking, alcohol consumption, and coffee drinking during Armenian memorials. For forty days, we catered to people, providing everything they needed to have an ideal "mourning." We supplied all sorts of top-shelf alcohol, varieties of food, and even expensive cigarettes for people to smoke their sorrows away. There was barely any time left in between for me to mourn my father's death with my family, as it should be. We weren't able to spend time together as a family to grieve the significant loss we had suffered. I was beginning to think that this whole month-long event was for others and less about my father's memory and his family.

People filled all of our bedrooms and common areas, leaving no space for me to be alone. Sometimes I would hide under the tables, escaping from everyone, and trying to find my own ways to cope in my attempted solitude. It was during one of my moments in hiding that I found out how much our house was worth and how big it was in terms of square feet. They spoke about my home as if they were discussing a property on the market at an open house. Those people were already talking about when and how our house would need to be sold. They were already under the assumption that we couldn't afford to keep our home and would most probably sell it in exchange for something smaller. They assumed our family wouldn't need nor be able to manage to keep a big house without a man providing for and protecting us. I don't think anyone in my family realized the level of offense some of our relatives displayed by overstepping their boundaries and sharing their unwanted opinions. I saw all of it even when they didn't.

When the grieving period ended and our relatives had no other reason to come over, we were finally alone. All of a sudden, our house became quiet, but my mother's crying did not cease. I would constantly hear her talking to my father in every portrait in every room of our house. There wasn't a day that went by without feeling the presence of my father's spirit by my side, and to this day, I refuse to let go of him. I want his spirit to stay with me for as long as I live. I need his strength and guidance when life is tough. I turn to him for help when I am going through hardships, and his energy always gives me a sense of safety and certainty. I still feel his existence, especially during life's most fragile moments.

Life does go on, but I believe there is no timeline for grief. I still grieve my father's death, and there is not a day that goes by that I don't miss him. I always wonder what life would be like if he was still here or lived just a few years longer. My father's death changed my life forever, and so did my perception of the world.

The wild predictions our relatives had about us not being able to stay in our house turned into reality, and my mother sold our home. I later found out she was looking to sell our house before my father's passing. When she first laid eyes on our house, she fell in love with its old Iranian architectural design. She especially fell for the big howz— a small round or square pool, typical of a Persian garden, like a Roman piscina. It was centrally located in the middle of the back yard with a shallow fountain inside. I can still remember that the howz was constructed of light and dark blue traditional mosaic in small square pieces. There were colorful goldfish in it all year round except during winters. Winter in Iran can be frigidly cold. I remember the backyard was well trimmed, flourishing with flowers and plants all around it. I have to credit my mother for this and her exceptional gardening skills. Her passion for planting beautiful flowers turned our backyard into a perfect traditional Persian garden.

My mother took great pride in purchasing the house with only two walkthroughs and couldn't wait to show it off to my father, who was out of town for work. Shortly after, she regretted her purchase due to its location, directly across the street from a large school with a big yard. That yard was surrounded by brick walls about five feet tall, facing our house. As tall as these brick walls were, they didn't seem to prevent the piles of school kids' leftover food from ending up on our property.

During this time, the Shah (The King of Iran) started a program to provide free daily meals for all children from kindergarteners to fourteen-year-olds. I believe It was part of the Shah's White Revolution, through which he was trying to reform the education system in Iran by providing more for less fortunate children. The government gave one-third of a pint of free milk, pistachios, fresh fruit, and biscuits to all children in Iran. This program covered all schools, both public and private.

Healthy and nutritious food was provided by the Shah's benevolent order, coming from a place of kindness, only to be thoughtlessly wasted by children. It seemed as though students in these schools were having their nutritional needs met someplace else. If a child were truly hungry, they would not waste a free meal provided for them. I remember I argued about this notion so many times in my life with many different people in my peer group. For some reason, I was most outraged at this purely shameful act of wasting perfectly good food. I couldn't comprehend how one could waste something as sacred as food when there are people who would be so grateful to have it.

Even the Armenian private school which I attended provided this free meal. I remember every day we would get the same triangle-shaped milk carton with a plastic straw, fruits of different varieties, and biscuits. The school that I was attending had strict disciplinary rules and regulations. We could not consume anything in the hallways or out of the cafeteria, and food was prohibited on the playground. We had to finish eating in our classroom or at the cafeteria before going out to play. The school near our house, however, lacked the kind of discipline we had at our school. The students from this school would throw milk all over the place and create chaos every day. Every single day we would clean and collect at least ten to twenty cartons of milk that landed in our back yard after the kids had their daily food fight. The students stomped on the unopened cartons of milk on the ground with all of their might. Milk stains were found in our backyard frequently accompanied by the white pungent odorous substance that found its way inside and out of our house. The school director's failure to take control of the situation resulted in sympathy being his only form of reparation.

Despite the remnants of the daily food fights, excessive noise, and somewhat displeasing ambiance around our property, we loved that house because of all the memories we created there. I would miss that house, but letting go of it was a different kind of pain for my mother, far different from mine. She couldn't bear the thought of living in that house any longer because she only loved that house with my father in it. When he left, he took her attachment to our home with him. She was looking to downsize the house and find a safer place for her children, but that was only part of the incentive to move. Her heart was not in that house anymore. She could no longer live in the home that she built with my father without him.

Saying goodbye to the house full of memories of my father was like saying goodbye to my safe place. I had emotional ties to my house, and it was always going to remain my home. I was five years old when we moved into that house, residing there from the beginning until the end of my childhood. I was worried about not being able to take all of my beautiful memories with me, but I had no other choice other than trying my best to take as much with me as I could. The time came for our farewells and to say goodbye to our house, neighborhood friends, and even to our tenants—whom I really didn't like. Our house was a three-story building and was way bigger than my family needed. So when we bought it, we rented out the first floor to another Armenian family. Taking my mother's word that our tenants were good people, the new owner allowed them to live there until they could find a new place to stay.

My mother liked the family living on the first floor and thought of them as a kind and responsible family despite my constant allegations against them. I am still sure that they are responsible for the disappearance of my pets. I knew they were the reason for the disappearance of my tiny yellow baby chicks. I had a big wooden box full of yellow chicks. I even had names for them and would put different colors of threads around their legs, calling them by the colors. I named them silly names like Green Leg, Red Cheeks, Blue Head, etc. They were my little pet chicks, and I loved them. Sometimes I would play with them for hours on end, not knowing where the time went. One day I noticed that a few of my chicks were missing. I immediately knew that our tenants were the ones to blame.

My mother always sympathized with me for the loss of my chicks, but I never got a sense of reassurance from her that she confronted our neighbors. She had experienced something similar in her early years of marriage while living in the same housing complex as her In-laws (my grandparents). My parents had a duck who was living in the pond in their backyard. This duck was considered their pet and was taken care of by my parents. They would feed it and tend to it when it looked like it needed help. One day my mother walked into the backyard and noticed that the duck was missing. She walked into the kitchen and saw that her mother-in-law was making Fesenjan stew. Fesenjan is a traditional Persian stew usually made with either duck or chicken, walnuts, pomegranate paste, and sugar. It is a very delicious meal with a sweet and savory taste. What wasn't so sweet about this specific stew was that her mother-in-law used my parents' pet duck as the meat source. Fesenjan is now my older son's favorite dish. However, I make it with chicken and not our household pets. My mother still remembers how her mother-in-law made fun of her refusal to sit at the dinner table where her pet duck had been served.

Moving to our new house in a new neighborhood was more effortless than I had anticipated, despite some emotional hurdles—at least the process of packing and unpacking all of our furniture and belongings. It felt like a time of new beginnings for me to let go of the past pain. It was a fresh start not only for me but especially for my mother. She decided to buy brand new furniture and appliances so she wouldn't have to carry that burden of losing her husband with her to our new house. We all gathered our irreplaceable personal belongings and a few kitchenware items and moved to our new home. The stress of moving furniture was taken off our shoulders, but we still had much to do when we moved in.

The first day of our move was a melting pot of emotions and the main one being that we were homesick. We liked our new house, but it was incomparable to our previous one. It was hard to look at this new place as our 'home'. We had to check out our new community and get to know our neighbors. It seemed like the neighbors had the same inclination as well. Although it was nice getting to know our new neighborhood, our neighbors' welcoming gestures were coming off as overbearing. I felt like the neighbors' kids were checking up on me at all times, making it very difficult to settle in comfortably. I was constantly feeling like the new kid in town, and that feeling was a reminder that this place was not my home. My mother, on the other hand, had done an excellent job of making her place in the town. She did such a fantastic job at convincing herself that she was exactly where she belonged that everyone else just treated her like she had been there for a long time. She was greeted warmly by the neighbors, called them by their first names, and was always making new friends during the neighborhood's morning coffee hour.

After just a few days in our new house, we learned that my brother living in the United States was in a terrible car accident. He was severely injured, but his injuries were thankfully not life-threatening. My brother had managed to walk away from terrible wreckage in one piece. We were so happy and grateful that God had spared his life. As a form of appreciation to God for saving my brother's life, we conducted Matagh. This is one of the most enticing yet gruesome traditions in the Armenian culture. The history behind the Matagh tradition precedes back to Armenia and its nations, dating back to 301 AD during the era of St. Gregory, the Illuminator. He was a patron saint as well as the first official figure of the Armenian Apostolic Church. He was imprisoned for over a decade by King Tiridates IV, the king of Arsacid Armenia. Eventually, St. Gregory converted the king and Armenia to Christianity. He then offered a thanksgiving sacrifice to God in the Church of

St. John the Forerunner, located in a city in Armenia named Taron.

This sacrifice consisted of slaughtering various animals and distributing the meat to the underprivileged. Matagh is essentially an offering; its meaning and symbolism serve as a gift to God as well as assisting the poor. The offering is carried out as a gesture of gratitude to God for saving a loved one from great misfortune or death. The animal usually chosen for sacrifice is a lamb. Once the animal has been sacrificed, the meat must be distributed right away, so it is fresh. Matagh also has several strict rules, and two of them state that it can not be conducted forty days before Easter and not on a Wednesday nor Friday.

Because our brother nearly lost his life, it was reasonable for us to conduct this matagh as a means of gratitude to God. The lamb was brought to our house and was tied up to a tree a few days before the actual matagh day. This was so it could be fattened up by overfeeding it. It was my chore to feed him and provide him with water. As if the poor animal understood that he was there to be slaughtered, he expressed distress by shaking his head around and trying to get loose from the rope. It was a painful sight to see an animal being held captive and tortured for the purpose of an offering.

We invited some relatives and hired a priest to conduct blessings and prayers on the day of the matagh. I did not like watching the life taken from an animal, so I was nowhere near the slaughtering ceremony when it was time. Needless to say, I did not eat even a small piece of lamb meat when it was cooked. I had built an emotional bond with the lamb during those three days I took care of it, and I felt sick even thinking about eating him. Some of the meat was distributed right away to our neighbors, and some of it was barbecued for the friends and relatives who were at our house. From what I can remember, my mother was very frustrated by my behavior that day. In her eyes, it was very disrespectful that I refused to help her distribute the meat among the neighbors and help on the day of the ceremony.

Thousands of memories were created while living in that house, yet I recall only a handful of them. If I could only travel and visit the actual house, perhaps my old memories could be retrieved, including all of the missing details. The memories that do come back to me vividly all relate to traumatic events, such as memories of the Iranian Revolution and the war between Iran and Iraq.

Chapter Four

HIGH SCHOOL

1978 was an important year, right before the Iranian Revolution, which consisted of the events that put an end to the secular monarchy in Iran. This occurred under the rule of the Shah, king of Iran, during the Pahlavi dynasty, and in its place came the Islamic Republic.

The start of high school was a big and exciting transition for me. New classes were filled with fresh faces on a new school campus. Getting used to this new version of normal was not easy for most, but for me, the puzzle pieces were fitting together effortlessly. The pace of my classes was not too difficult for me to keep up with, partly due to my love for school and education. I truly enjoyed going to school and learning more about every subject. I did not have to go out of my way to find friends either. I made them naturally, partly because I did not like the idea of putting on a facade to gain the approval or friendship of others. I was at all times, Violet.

Adapting to this new social atmosphere by making new friends and establishing a crowd with whom I fit in made me feel like I found a place where I belonged. I was so content with how my high school experience was starting off that I began diverting my efforts onto something else. I began to pay more attention to my interests and hobbies, focusing on the things that came more naturally, such as my social life or academics. I wanted to find my calling and what drove me to be the most motivated version of myself. I found this through the arts of theater and literature. After school, my mom would take me to our local recreation center, where there were bountiful extracurricular activities ranging from sports to art. The interest that was at the top of my priorities was theater, and despite not always getting cast as the starring role or even one that I enjoyed, I never abandoned it.

I used to really enjoy reading and acting because it placed me in this fictional bubble where I would forget about who I was, where I came from, and who I wanted to become. It took away all the pressures I had as a young girl growing up in a country where each tomorrow was unpredictable. It made me happy to have control over this aspect of my life. After all, life is what you make of it, and we must live our lives the way we envision in our dreams. That is why I strongly believe we should structure our lives the way we want to and do the things that are worthwhile for us. For me, that was becoming one with all of my storybook characters and the roles that I had to play. Still, after all these years, I look back, and I exhale with pride that I went after everything that I wanted, whether it worked out in my favor or not. I did it all in my own special way and only my way.

My high school was a relatively new building that didn't look like a school from the outside. It had very large classrooms filled with long communal tables where the students' spots were first come, first served. The students would often fight over who got to sit by the window, and it was always the person who claimed it first. It was attached to the Armenian Apostolic Church, separated by a metal fence that was too strong to budge. The metal bars on this fence were spaced only about 10 inches apart. It did not take long for me to discover that it was an escape route for the rebellious upper-grade students. Some of the female students with smaller body frames could easily squeeze through the fence and make their way to the other side of the school, ending up in the churchyard. With the influence of peer pressure and a hint of curiosity, I found myself using the same escape route along with those rebellious kids, just a few months into the school year. Although this was a very clever way for most of the girls to escape, the boys preferred a different method due to their larger body size. One would jump over the fence and then hold a hook for the rest to jump over.

It may have been considered defiant to ditch school while class was in session, but my reason for doing so was a bit different than the rest of my classmates. I would escape to go to church, especially on Saturdays or Sundays. I enjoyed stopping by for a quick prayer and candle lighting whenever I had the chance to leave without the risk of getting caught. Living in a Muslim country, it was mandatory that all people observe Islamic holidays, including Christians. The schools and businesses were in session on Saturdays and Sundays, with Fridays being our only day off.

The last class of the day was PE, otherwise known as Physical Education. PE was a dedicated time for us to do any type of sport or activity that would pass for physical education, only if the students participated, of course. Usually, this was whatever sport that fit our liking, and for me, it was basketball. This was my go-to sport growing up, but only if I was lucky enough to find a court available to play on. So basically, we were on our own, left in the courtyard with minimal supervision during the last hour of the school day. It was always around this time when the boys were conveniently nowhere to be found; therefore, physically unable to participate in physical education. After noticing this oddly non-coincidental trend, I figured out that the boys would end their days early and hop over the fence to play billiards at a place nearby.

Something about billiards was intriguing to me, and I was always curious to learn how to play, so I learned the technique behind the sport. However, billiards was never readily available for a young girl like me. Every time I saw the boys leaving for their daily billiard trip, I would ask them if I could come with them, but the answer was always no. I could not wait for the day when they would let me accompany them. "Someday, we will take you with us," my two close male classmates would always promise me. The reason the boys always turned me down when I would ask to join, was because this place, and pretty much any other billiard place, mostly catered to men. Since Iranian-Armenian culture was very traditional, activities were strictly separated by gender. This meant it wasn't socially acceptable for girls to take part in activities designated for men and vice versa.

The more I asked, the more excuses they came up with as a way of protecting me from this overly masculine and significantly sexist place. I had asked so often that I was becoming an annoyance to these boys. But finally, the long-awaited day came for me to join the boys in going to the billiard place with one of my girlfriends and a few of those rebellious schoolboys. The pool hall looked nothing like what I was anticipating. It was minimally illuminated and had a gut-wrenching odor that only got worse as time progressed. This repulsively displeasing atmosphere made it hard for me even to remember why I was there in the first place—to play pool. I could not bear being there even before the start of the first game, but I did not want to be the one to ruin the outing for my friends, so we stayed.

They say sometimes you find yourself in the wrong place at the wrong time, and this was one of those occasions. After a few games of pool and fed up with that vile odor marinating in every crevice of my nasal cavities, we stepped out of the billiard place to head home. As we walked out of the main entrance, we opened the door to a historical movement unfolding before our very eyes—a sight that made it one of the most unforgettable days of my life—making every single detail a vivid recollection. I agonized over what I saw. The street was blocked with hundreds of thousands of protesters. We knew that Tehran and surrounding cities were at their breaking point regarding the regime and Anti-Royalists were rioting almost every day and everywhere, but this was a sight I had never seen before.

Massive demonstrations had begun across the country. Liberals, leftist Marxists, and clergymen were all united. Many had nothing in common besides the opportunistic interest in allying themselves with their peers for the sake of participating in a grand movement. It was easily presumed through their transparency, that if any of them rose to power, they would be relentless until they successfully abolished the country's predecessors. Watching these demonstrations grow in population and intensity caused uncertainty and anxiety amongst my family and relatives. Some fled the country, and some, including my mother, were so overcome with disbelief that they were in denial. But the disastrous Revolution was unprecedented and was rapidly progressing each day. Since the Shah had immense regard for human life, he did not want to resort to bloodshed to keep his crown. In the book, The Shah, written by Abbas Milani, a quote by Shah, reads, "A Sovereign may not save his throne by shedding his countryman's blood."

The demonstrators broke out in many different cities before they hit the biggest city and the capital of Iran, Tehran. Riots had been sweeping through Tehran for a few months now, leaving everyone with tremendous confusion about the state of our country. Nobody from the younger demographics knew the severity of it all, but judging by how our hometown was burning down to ashes in front of our eyes, we knew deep down how bad it was. Grown-ups would remind us about the country being tumultuous, and we should take extra caution when going out anywhere. If my mother were to find out that I left school without her permission in a taxi, she would have been more than disappointed. Being an impulsive child who was enticed by adventure, disappointing my mother wasn't a thought that crossed my mind at the moment.

Our main concern was figuring out how to get out of the center of the chaos without getting hurt. We had no idea how serious the hostility was of the protesters in opposition to the current monarchial government until we were caught in the middle of it. Vandalism, cars on fire, angry protesters shouting to get their voices heard, and unpleasant body language. They were demanding things that I had never heard in my life. "Death to Imperialists," "Death to Shah." They would chant these phrases at the top of their lungs, but I still couldn't comprehend why they were saying it. We had to get out of there and head back to school as soon as possible because I had to take the school bus home. The road back to school was closed due to an abundance of rioting protesters. We were scrambling, trying to find a passage to take us to a familiar area in an attempt to steer clear from danger. Instead, we ended up in an unfamiliar street in a strange part of town.

I was already very skeptical, but something caught my attention that sent chills down my spine. Graffiti in the form of a large mural that said: "Armenians take your Shah and leave our country" I never thought of myself as a foreigner until that moment. The Armenians living in Iran never considered themselves foreigners because we had been there for so many generations that it became our homeland just as much as Armenia. Iran is our country, and we were always treated equally and even sometimes surprisingly favorable. Armenian history in Iran precedes many centuries in time, but all it took was for that moment, for me, to question the truth of my reality.

The typical November cold day felt even colder than usual. The piercing wind was traveling along my spine, causing shivering I never thought would end. It was hard to believe that just a few hours earlier, I had simply been looking forward to a long-awaited game of billiards and ending up in this problematic situation. It dawned on me that I had forgotten my jacket at school. There was no way I could go back for my jacket or find a spare one during this mess of a time. The weather wasn't the only thing making me cold, but also the uncertainty of what was to come struck trembles in my heart.

That afternoon I arrived home very late and managed to convince my mother that I had missed my school bus and had to take a cab home. I left the details out so she could fill them in—however they made sense in her head—in hopes of avoiding as much trouble as possible. Making it home and putting my cold purple-tinted feet and hands on a heater was bliss. We had a big heater in the corner of our living room where we would gather around on cold days and catch up on each other's days. Having this time to spend with family gave me a sense of security and warmth, almost to the point of sharing the crazy day I had. I was scared they would judge me for my choice deeming it as irresponsible, so I shared nothing from that day. As an adolescent, it was hard to earn a sense of trust from parents, but I had accomplished it and did not want to jeopardize that.

That evening was the beginning of my chronic nightmares which lasted longer than they should have. On that very first night, which was most likely a result of my traumatic incident I had experienced that day, I had sleepwalked to my sisters' room. My sisters were awakened in terror to see me just aimlessly walking around their beds. I had no recollection of this, so the next day, my sisters told me I had sleepwalked to them in the middle of the night, asking them to put their head down on the table to listen to the voices. They asked me if I remembered anything, and I honestly responded that I didn't, even though I could think of an event that troubled me enough to sleepwalk. I was already coming down with a cold and a high fever, and they figured my fever was the thing to blame for my strange behavior. I missed school for a few days due to my bronchitis.

I shook off my cold and bronchitis in just a few days, but the Revolution left a mark in my life that could never be forgotten. A deep mark, consisting of riots happening in front of my eyes. This resulted in a complete shift of my reality from my adjusting to the norms of a different religion. Sadly, my generation of Iranians sacrificed many irreplaceable childhood years in exchange for just being present during the Revolution. Of course, I was too young to participate in any protests or movements, but I was on the sidelines, experiencing it as a young girl. Sometimes I wonder how it would be if my destiny could be rewritten, and my fate was different. How different would I be as a person if I grew up in a peaceful country free from war and conflict? I know for certain my life as a young girl would be much more normal, but normal isn't always the best. My life growing up in Iran has contributed to my strength and ability to experience the unexpected. The ability to make the most out of the circumstances that I have been given, in itself, makes me who I am.

Chapter Five

GERMANY

As living conditions became less sustainable in my country, I became increasingly determined to turn my hopes of emigrating to another country into reality. It came as no surprise that I was not the only one trying to leave Iran due to the revolution's chaotic upheaval. Unfortunately, it wasn't likely that everyone who desired to leave the country would be provided that opportunity. In order to leave, we needed to apply for a VISA through the embassy of the country we desired to travel to as a gateway to America.

Due to the American Embassy's non-operative status in Iran, the most common place people applied for a VISA was to European countries. Obtaining a VISA for one of these countries was rare due to the high volume of people trying to exit Iran concurrently. The chances of beginning the VISA process were so slim that it was almost necessary to have some sort of personal relationship with an operative of the European embassy. Usually, the closest one would get was knowing someone who also knew someone with ties to this embassy employee. This person who was in contact with the embassy was the one who would work as the middleman between the two parties.

Of course, an advantage like this was not an inexpensive and realistic solution for everyone, but I am grateful to say it was for my sister Jenik and me. Our family friend knew someone who introduced us to a third-party individual who would transfer our papers to the German embassy. This process cost my mother a mortgage on our house, which didn't even guarantee our approval, but nonetheless, my sister and I were lucky once again. We received our approval and were cleared to leave Iran. We said goodbye to our mother and our other sister Juliet at the airport, feeling saddened that we were leaving our loved ones and homeland behind. Despite these last-minute bitter emotions, we still had the sweet taste of anticipating the road ahead.

Our friend Klara ended up getting her VISA approved for Germany as well, so she accompanied us on this journey. At this point, it was Jenik, Klara, and me, against the world. I was 19, my sister was six years ahead of me, and our first major event as adults was moving to a brand new foreign country. The journey from Iran to Germany was extremely eventful and yet only the beginning of an even more colorful story to come. This chapter of my life started with the three of us boarding our plane, covered up conservatively with our tunic and head garments known as hijab. (The hijab is an Islamic woman's head covering, generally a veil or a scarf worn in public). Reluctant to catch ourselves in legal trouble, we were still behaving accordingly with the rules of modesty that were enforced in Iran. By the time our plane landed in Germany, however, we were tunic-free, and our hair rested on our backs, free from the constraints of our hijabs.

Our appearance being so different, and our spirit reborn as liberated women, the flight attendant struggled to recognize us at first glance. She humorously stated that the plane would turn back around because we broke the dress code—according to an Iranian Muslim man who would escort us back home. Knowing how ridiculous this sounded made it that much more terrifying if it turned out to be true. After seeing our joyous faces quickly switch to terror, the flight attendant promptly said she was kidding, turning that scare into a humorous moment.

Upon our arrival in Germany, we were greeted at the airport by a friend from back home, accompanied by his new German girlfriend. He was the only familiar face we knew in Germany and was there for the same reason that we were. Preferring a friend's company, we had planned for him to pick us up and take us to the place we would call our temporary home. But seeing my friend and this unfamiliar girl walking closer to us only led to one thought racing through my mind; he has a girlfriend waiting for him back home. This was our first encounter on German soil, and it was our admired childhood friend, betraying his girlfriend by coming here to welcome us with another girl by his side. It was gut-wrenching. Upon approaching them, I couldn't help but greet them with a cold "hello." It wasn't my place to intervene, but I kept picturing his girlfriend back home, counting down the days until they could meet again. She was the one with whom he had made future plans and promised her that they would reunite while still maintaining the relationship.

His disgraceful action was so morally conflicting with my belief system that it was unbearable. I had hoped he was at least conscious that his wrongdoing would eventually hurt and break one if not both of these girls' hearts. As wrong as it was, it was slightly impressive for an immigrant of only a few months to be caught in an affair. "She is helping me with my German language," he blurted out as he noticed my mood going increasingly dull during our encounter. The guilt was starting to seep through his eyes as he restlessly continued justifying what his relationship with this girl was, in Armenian, of course. Fatigued from lack of sleep during our long flight, I maintained the thought that someone's love affair was the least of my concerns, so I took what I saw that day and locked it up in memories I never wanted to revisit.

Exhausted from the incredibly long and tiring flight, my only longing was a nice warm shower. My anticipation quickly turned as sour as spoiled milk as our friend said we were headed straight to the refugee camp. "Refugee what?" I said in confusion, doubting my ears' ability because of what they just heard. Refugee camps were typically for people planning on gaining permanent residency in Germany. He knew our journey must continue to the United States, so why was he taking us to a refugee camp? "This has got to be a mistake," I thought to myself as my anxiety heightened, and my need for sleep faded drastically. He continued to explain that we needed to stay in Germany longer than our visa permitted, so it would be necessary to stay at the camp. Thirty days was not enough time for us to obtain a US residency or green card, which we knew before we came.

What was not so clear was the part where we had to live at these refugee camps practically against our own will. I had envisioned something more like a long-term hotel stay, but that was just optimism and wishful thinking. After hitting us with this harsh reality, he reminded us that we were not there for pleasure but more like business. We had a goal to fulfill and were still taking the first steps of our journey, nowhere near the end yet. Instead of the fancy German hotel with nice showers in my daydreams, we were escorted to our temporary refugee camp housing near Frankfurt. At this point, we were well aware of what our living condition was going to be like during our stay in Germany. There were no luxurious showers and commodities, but instead, a very average housing situation located in this camp.

That was the only option available because traveling with a VISA made you a liability to the government. It was mandatory to live in these government-sanctioned houses for the first month of residency in Germany. This promoted organization of the people awaiting their paperwork for America by keeping them nearby. Those who wanted to live in Germany permanently had to provide a reason for their immigration, which was usually adverse treatment due to religious discrimination from their own country's government. That did not apply to us since permanent residency in Germany was never an option and would not become one. Staying close to family was always something my father valued, and it was always his long-term dream for the family to remain united. To honor his wishes, our plan was to eventually reunite in the United States and create the prosperous life we were unable to have back home.

As we waited for our immigration papers to process, our days in Germany consisted of trying to make our time there worthwhile and productive, all without establishing a permanent sense of home. Language proficiency was always necessary for me, so even knowing that my stay in Germany was temporary, I found it a priority to learn the native language. I signed up at a community college nearby to learn as much German as possible, given the short amount of time I had there. I loved learning, and school was always enjoyable for me. It was naturally ingrained in my blood to expand my educational horizons, and I took every opportunity that would allow me to do that even in a brand new, unfamiliar country.

Lockdown enforced at the main gates was set strictly for 8 pm every night because it was government-enforced housing. One would assume this would feel almost like imprisonment, but not for me. I saw this as a new set of rules that I had the opportunity to break. The legal drinking age was 18. My friend Klara and I were 19 at the time, so you can see where this is headed. Clubbing would have been hard with the lockdown hours, so Klara and I would jump the gate that closed at 8 pm, and our nighttime adventures began. Sometimes our outings would last until the crack of dawn and consist of dancing, German disco music, and unforgettable memories with people we were never going to see again.

We were very responsible for being just 19 and 25 years old, so we never got into any serious problems. The location at which we were staying near Frankfurt was so safe that finding ourselves in trouble wasn't a worry for us. I was much more thrill-seeking as a young woman, which explains why the adrenaline rush of light-hearted delinquency was so appealing. Despite our eventful nights out, I was always a little more cautious than those around me. My sense of responsibility didn't disappear under any circumstances. I would never classify myself as a troublemaker by nature, but that didn't mean I had to be boring either.

Growing up in Iran, most people I was acquainted with were Iranian Armenians, making an encounter with someone from a different background an entirely new experience. Near the apartment where we stayed was an American military base, which I walked past every day. During my daily walk to the city, one of the military guards standing outside the base caught my attention. We would exchange smiles often, and through our limited exchanges, we became friends.

My English fluency was not up to par with this soldier, and neither of us spoke German well, making our interactions on a very surface level, but unique. Despite our limited ability to communicate, we always invited him over for afternoon Armenian coffee. Sometimes the energy of a person is so pleasant, its effect surpasses the need for verbal communication. We spent many afternoons having coffee and just enjoying each other's presence. However, all good things must come to an end, as did our friendship with this soldier. When it came time for our departure to America, we had no means of contacting this man, so we left without saying our final goodbyes.

The only memory regarding the camp was the adventurous memories created within their very walls, and their "brotchen" bread and Nutella served for breakfast in the cafeteria. However, don't be fooled by the free breakfast. Pretty much everything else served at the cafeteria was repulsive and nearly inedible. When I wasn't jumping over fences and breaking curfew with Klara, I was trying to steer clear from the crazy girl that shared a room with the three of us. I did not know much about mental illness at the time, but I knew for a fact that the crazy girl whom we shared a room with had some type of mental disorder. She had a deep ill-founded hatred for me, and I was never able to comprehend what I had done to be treated like the enemy. I soon realized that this was not my fault and indeed a result of her own mental distress. I genuinely believe that there was something this girl possessed internally that altered her perception of me. She was friendly with me until she decided I was her enemy.

Her issue with me was that I distanced myself from her and did not give her much attention. How could I be anywhere but on civil terms with someone who went from being an acquaintance to potentially plotting my death within a matter of minutes? Some days I would get smiles and "How are you?" and other days get death stares and accusatory statements about why I didn't like her. My sister was always better at putting up with difficult people, so our roommate felt unthreatened by her. She often even confided in her and told her about the hatred she had for me. Sometimes I slept in my friend Klara's bed because it was further away from this crazy roommate, and I felt more secure knowing I wasn't alone. I could sleep peacefully that way without fear of this girl strangling me to death. She looked very capable of it too. Besides our roommate however, the conditions at this place started to appear increasingly unsafe. I felt inclined to apply for a new apartment.

After spending so much time in the housing office

requesting a relocation, the camp director and I ended up on a first-name basis. After various attempts and much pleading, I was finally able to get us all approved for new housing not too far from the camp. Shortly after our approval, we moved, and I was very content with the new apartment because it was much cleaner and was free from crazy roommates and residents. For some reason, no matter where you go, it is inevitable to have at least one bad experience. In our case, the downside to our apartment, was the fact that there were rather sneaky neighbors who managed to steal our packages. They were sneaky because we never caught them doing it, but we were almost certain that they lived amongst us.

International distribution of money was prohibited, so my mother would find ways to send us an allowance we used for our living essentials. She put gold coins in the lid of deodorant or perfume bottles so they would not be confiscated. She packed these with dried nuts and fruit to give us a sweet treat to enjoy a part of the home that was missing from our lives. Being the naive young girl that I was, I shared my excitement with the neighbors that our mother sent us currency in gold coins. It was so rare for families to send each other money, that my intention of showing off turned into an act of self-sabotage. I don't know who ended up stealing our coins, but after I told our secret to several of our neighbors, our next gold coin package went missing.

Everything was so orderly and well organized for us, making my time in Germany a sweet memory. This new country that was becoming my temporary home was not only angelic to the naked eye but sweet and pleasant to all the senses. From the smell of fresh pastries and bread baked from scratch every morning to the aromatic floral soap, I would use every day. But no matter how perfect Germany was, my heart kept longing for my real home— Iran. Germany's weather was always so cold, and it snowed frequently, but that wasn't unfamiliar to me. Walking knee-deep in the snow to reach my destination for the day reminded me of all the snow days in Iran when we would walk to the school bus stop in our tall snow boots. My hometown was always in the back of my mind, and everything I experienced in this new country served as a reminder of the place I had to leave behind.

At the time, German culture was still closed-minded, to say the least, regarding prejudiced acts towards immigrants. Discrimination was something I had the misfortune of being accustomed to after seeing it happen in front of me on multiple occasions. Being fair-skinned with lighter hair granted you a discrimination-free pass. This was how it was for me, but unfortunately, not for my sister. She was darker than me with black hair and a distinct ethnic appearance, a dead giveaway that she was a foreigner. She would get pushed and shoved in the metro in evidently intentional ways. Although it was never anything more severe than that, the way that people would treat us was too distinct to be overlooked.

For a country's people who seemed to be closed-minded regarding foreign encounters, sexual modesty did not seem to be a priority. I remember going to a beach famous for its clothing guidelines, or lack of, rather. I went to my first ever nude beach, and it was the first and probably the only thing that did not remind me of back home. It was a lot for me to take in both visually and mentally for various reasons. The main one was that I grew up in such a conservative society, one which had women cover up from nearly head to toe to leave the house. And if you didn't, it could have resulted in punishment or arrest. This freedom level was not easy for me to readily comprehend due to the drastic difference in normality that I was used to back home. My friends and I wore bathing suits and received many dirty looks from the nude participants. Needless to say, I never had the desire to return there.

While I was going to school in Germany, I met a few Persian students who were just like me, in a sense. They were all individuals who had grown up with different beliefs and political backgrounds, but all found themselves living in Germany. I became very close with a girl named Nazanin. Her brother was a pilot, tragically murdered after the start of the Revolution for being an avid supporter of the Shah, the King of Iran. Nazanin was a year younger than me, but this was such a minimal age difference, especially because we connected on so many levels. She was well versed in history and politics, and we had a lot in common. The thing that bonded us together was how much we missed our home. I loved spending time with her and having someone to talk to during such a transitional period in my life. Together we cried, laughed, and ate as much German chocolate as our stomachs could handle. Nazanin was a reserved person and did not socialize much, especially when we were around other Persian students. Her reticent demeanor and personality were a result of her restricted life in Iran. She blamed the Islamic government for all of the hardships she and her family had endured. Unfortunately, I lost contact with her after she moved to Sweden to live with her relatives.

Iran had undergone profound changes after the Islamic Revolution in 1979 and had destroyed many children's most crucial years, including Nazanin's and mine., It was during my early teens when the Islamic Revolution struck a desire in me to leave the country as soon as I was an adult. Some were living in exile because their political beliefs had forced them to flee the country. I did not know much about any political parties other than the constitutional monarchy. After all, I was born and grew up in the Shah (King of Iran's) era. Nazanin's knowledge and experience of Iran were almost identical to mine, and it was almost as if fate had brought us together.

My experience living in Germany allowed me to appreciate life's simplest wonders in any way they are presented. I did not expect my journey to America to involve living in Europe, but this was an experience that I was meant to have. I learned the meaning of a different kind of independence. The type where you have to fend for yourself in a completely unfamiliar place, uncertain of what tomorrow holds. All the people I met along the way have impacted my life in one way or another. Whether that be the American soldier who taught me that human interaction is less complex than we had imagined or Nazanin, who made me feel less alone in a time of uncertainty. I was grateful for all of it.

Author Violet (second from left) and siblings posing for a picture (Circa 1960s)

Tina - Violet (left) and her childhood Iranian friend Tina who shared no common language with at the time. They were always happy to see each other. (Circa 1960s)

Dad - Violet's dear father in his early years
(Circa 1940s)

Violet's father making time in his busy constructing schedule to smile for a picture with his work truck. (Circa 1960s)

Living the Hollywood Dream. Violet having headshots taken for her modeling portfolio.

MD Travel
321 S. BRAND BLVD. • GLENDALE, CA 91204

• FAX
Pgr.

Violet Baghdasarian
Travel Consultant

Violet's business card for when reality hit and modeling failed and she started her second job at a travel agency.

Violet in her early twenties rocking her typical hair and makeup style.

Violet's wedding - October 4, 2003

Violet and her mother - Wedding October 4, 2003

Violet at home in Malibu, CA USA

Chapter Six

THE PLAN

The plan was to move to America before I started school as a little girl. My father was always in search of the best and safest country to move his family to. Despite Iran being known as the "an Island of stability" at the time, his belief maintained that Christians must live in a Christian country. However, Armenians never felt threatened during the Pahlavi Regime, and it didn't occur to them, including my family, that they were being treated differently. We lived in an Armenian community, were a part of Armenian clubs, and attended Armenian private schools.

None of this seemed to satisfy my Father's appetite for growth and accomplishment with regard to his big dream. He was looking to establish a safe and stable life for his family in the most optimal way he could and had this vision of relocating the family to America. He always talked about it, especially when my mom's sister married an American working in Iran on a work contract. I remember that their wedding took place at the American Embassy. It was indoors, but from what I remember as a little girl, the floor looked like green grass. In reality, it was the facade of a beautifully green carpet.

My dad wanted to send my brother to live with my aunt and attend college in America, with the rest of us following shortly after. A new transition was upcoming for my brother, as his move to study in America was finalized. The topic of moving to America became a frequently discussed matter in our house after my brother was planning to move there. My father's family were discussing a move elsewhere. They were considering the possibility of moving to Armenia and establishing their lives there. Armenia was in a totally different condition at that time. It was a part of the Soviet Union's territory. The Soviet Union established Armenia as a country under their rule, and ultimately changed its title to the Armenian Soviet Socialist Republic. They had a mission to get Armenians living elsewhere to return to their country of ethnic origin.

My father's sister was trying to convince my dad to join her and her family in Armenia. My father didn't want to live in a country where civil rights were severely limited, and the regard for human life was diminished. Or in a place where the country's populace was mobilized in support of a single state ideology and the Communist Party's policies. He believed communism could easily fool poor people, not because they are unintelligent but because communism sounded so appealing in its promise of fair and reasonable treatment. He believed communism causes idleness and laziness in people. My father was an ambitious person and experienced the success of hard work, so this concept was of no appeal to him. Armenia was out of the question for us because of my father's wishes, but unfortunately, he couldn't talk his sister's family out of it.

According to Soviet officials, 250,000 Armenians have gone back to Armenia from different areas worldwide in the past 65 years. This migration was mainly in the 1920s and the years immediately following World War II. Roughly another 20,000 went back in 1970, the year in which my father's sister, her family, and a few of his friends and cousins migrated to Armenia. I remember the day of their departure. We were all gathered at the train station for the final farewell. Passengers were leaving Iran for a country that they had never visited nor had even stepped foot in and had no grasp of what the country was like. Fantasy and false advertisement deceived them into leaving their birthplace to head off to an unknown land. It was a sad day for young people who did not want to leave and for women who were forced by their husbands to go. The echo of screaming and crying took over the train station, making it an unpleasant place to be. Children being pushed onto the train against their will was a horrifying scene that I can still remember. My heart ached for them because I knew they were embarking on a journey that would give them no option to come back and visit their hometown.

Every passenger had a sad and uncertain expression on their face, not knowing what the future had in store. Life would be different at the end of that train ride, as I'm sure they knew. I am sure each one of them had their own reasons behind their departure. Some because they wanted to be in their Motherland, residing in the place of their ethnic origin. Some didn't want their kids to be associated with Persians. Some were in favor of Socialism and perceived equality in Armenia. The rest were just unfortunately deceived by the false promises made to them of a better life. For whatever reason, I was glad that I was not accompanying them on that train. Armenians emigrating from Iran were required to turn in their Iranian citizenship to the Iranian government, meaning they could never return to Iran.

We knew we would never see my aunt and her family again as it was a one-way trip for them, and they had no eligibility to return. I was only six years old, but I still remember the sorrow and sadness in the atmosphere mixed with the heavy smoke coming from the train, the smell of sweaty people, and wet crying faces everywhere. At every corner, there were emotional goodbyes, all involving two things: crying and hugging. Teenagers were trying to run away from the uncertain future awaiting them at the end of the train tracks, but their effort was futile. Their families were forcing them into the train cabins by pulling their hands while they were begging to stay with their relatives. One of my father's friends promised to tell him everything about life on the other side of the walls under Soviet Union rule. They created secret codes to use in these conversations since they already knew every phone conversation, and any letters coming out of the Soviet Union were hacked. Sadly, most of the time, the hacking was done by the neighbors.

The sad truth about conditions in Armenia was written in a letter received a few months after the departure of my dad's friend. He stated that they arrived safely and thanked him for the sweater he had given him, but the sweater was tight and felt suffocating. He wished he could return the sweater, but he could not get a refund. This was his code way of saying that life on the other side was not suitable but could not be undone.

This was at the time when Mohamad Reza Shah, aka The Shah, was ruling Iran. The Shah rose to power after his father was forced to step down. Reza Shah was the founder of the Pahlavi Dynasty. He rose from the ranks to become minister of the war, prime minister, and ultimately, the Shah of Iran. As a reformer/dictator, he laid the foundation of modern Iran. My father was born into the time when Reza Shah was the ruler of our country.

Reza Shah was my father's example of an idealistic ruler. He told us a story repeatedly until we knew the words verbatim, but we still loved hearing it again. The story goes that one day during his reign, Reza Shah was on a walk when he stumbled upon a craftsman who was working on one of his buildings. The worker was carving a lion holding up a pillar, and he noticed that the lion had crossed eyes. After addressing the issue with the craftsman, the response was, "Your eyes would be crossed too if you had to carry the weight of this pillar on your shoulder." The craftsman turned around and identified the man he encountered as The Reza Shah, himself! Of course, he apologized for his ignorance, but the Shah liked his impromptu answer and let him go unpunished. He even paid him a few gold coins for his hard work.

My father told us many stories about the royals and loved to talk about politics. He was an avid follower of the current newspaper and kept my mom up to date without her asking since her interest in politics was lacking. He would talk about how Reza Khan, later Reza Shah Pahlavi, was born in the Caspian province of Mazandaran. He lost his father in infancy, and at the age of 14, he chose a military career in the Persian Cossack Brigade, which was under the command of Russian officers. He was highly intelligent but had no formal education. In fact, he was so bright that an abundance of information wasn't necessary for him to come to a conclusion, and he was accustomed to westernization without travel to western nations. Besides being intelligent, the Reza Shah was also very sensitive. It was evident that he was displeased by the country's despicable condition and its army ever since his youth. As a soldier, he took part in many military ordeals, but what bothered him most was that he was under foreign officers' command.

After the Russian Revolution, some of the Russian officers in the brigade left, but the White Russians, who could not go with them, remained in command. In 1920, Reza led his fellow Persian officers to oust the Russians, becoming the brigade commander himself. Reza Shah built a strong modern army, subdued rebellious tribes, and instilled a sense of peace and security, which the country was desperate for and hadn't had for over a century. Ahmad Shah, the last of the Qajar Kingdom, was so overshadowed by the popular Rezah Khan that he permanently moved to Europe.

The creation of a Republic in Turkey influenced many Persians, including Reza Khan. At one point in time, there was even a movement to create a Republic in Iran. It soon became evident that although Persians did not mind having another ruler, they were reluctant to move away from a monarchical system. So, Parliament deposed the absent Ahmad Shah and proclaimed Reza Khah as the Shahanshah (King of Kings) of Iran. Therefore, being a pro-Westernized ruler favoring Western ideals, Rezah Shah issued a decree called Kashf-e-hijab, which banned the wearing of Islamic veils, headscarves, and chadors, as well as many types of traditional male clothing. This edict was swiftly and forcefully implemented. He also broke the radical reforms that had been a source of turbulence to the nation, disarming and partly settling them.

During the Shah's reign, educational and judicial reforms were in effect, laying grounds for establishing a modern state that reduced religion's influence. A wide range of legal affairs that had previously been the purview of Shi'a religious courts was now either administered by secular courts or overseen by state bureaucracies. As a result of this, the status of women in the country improved. The customary regulation of women wearing veils was banned. The marital age requirement was raised for women, and strict religious divorce laws that invariably favored men were made more equitable. The number and availability of secular schools increased for both boys and girls, and the University of Tehran was established. This new transformative ruler adopted modernization and secularization, which, in my opinion, altered the state of the country for the better.

The Shah built the Trans-Iranian Railway and started branch lines towards principal cities. He took control of the country's finances and communications, which up until the point before his rule had been in foreign hands. He built roads, schools, hospitals, opened the first university, and provided financial support for women to study abroad, creating new opportunities for women. This included granting the right to vote, the right to education, salaries equivalent to men, and the right to hold public office. But soon after the Shah paved the way for women to reach a state of equality, this crumbled, and his efforts went down the drain. Most of these rights were demolished after the Islamic Revolution, and the nation took many steps back and regressed from the new laws.

Women were not considered equal under Iran's constitution, adopted after the Islamic Revolution in 1979, which mandates legal code to Sharia Law and still exists in 2020. Abiding by this law, women are treated as half a man; men inherit twice what a woman would, and compensation for a woman's death is half of a man's. Iranian law still favors men, but the only difference now is that women are allowed to drive, attend University, and hold public office. Whenever I read about Iranian history, it greatly disturbs me that a government can dictate what a woman can wear. I cannot fathom how a government thinks controlling a woman's actions adds to their perceived power. A country should not dictate if a woman should leave her house covered up or not. The choice should lay in the hands of the woman herself. That is an ideal that the Shah upheld during his reign, which was an example of the Western sense of equality in which he believed.

Chapter Seven

AMERICA

The time had come for us to wave our days in Germany goodbye, and the long-awaited next chapter of our lives had finally arrived. My sister and I had moved to the United States of America, the final destination of our journey (or so I thought). We had to leave all of our memories and newfound home behind and begin from scratch once again. Unfortunately, this meant saying goodbye to our friend Klara as well. She didn't come to the states with us because she had no immediate family in America to sponsor her relocation. It was hard to say goodbye to someone who had been such a prominent part of my life, but we promised to assist her current status as an immigrant and keep in touch.

We headed to America without knowing what we had in store for us in this giant land of opportunity. On the day of our exit, I had many mixed emotions occupying every cell in my body. We said farewell once again to the little community we had built for ourselves, our friend Klara, and to the country that accepted us with open arms and took us under their wing. The country for which I would be forever grateful and indebted to. The level of hospitality and the country's safety as a whole made it feel like the closest place to home I could have been.

It was a cold and dark winter day when our plane landed in New York. Our flight to El Paso, Texas, got canceled due to unsafe flying conditions provoked by the harsh winter weather. The airline was kind enough to provide us a voucher for a nearby Hotel. It was not a five-star hotel of course, but it was a warm place with two double beds and getting some rest in a warm bed with clean sheets was all we needed. Our flight was dependent on how the weather was going to be like the next day, but we didn't worry. It was cold and dark outside to the point that touring the beautiful city was of no interest to us. The weather, however, wasn't the only thing holding us back. Our hotel was near the JFK Airport, which wasn't an ideal area for two young girls to stroll after dark. We had heard of nothing but insidious crimes and unpleasant news about New York City, which made it difficult for us to savor the experience.

We went to our room and stacked all of our luggage by the door, thinking that this would protect us in case we had a break-in. The next morning, we woke up, and luckily the luggage remained intact and the weather was in much better condition for our flight. We left New York for El Paso, Texas, aiming to finally reunite with our brother as well as my aunt and her family. As we finally arrived at this geographically isolated city bordering Juarez, Mexico, I was blindsided by its first impression. The city where we arrived was drastically different than any city in which I had ever lived. It was an abandoned desert, and the atmosphere of the natives was painfully dissimilar. The only sense of nostalgia I have traced back to this place was being close to my brother and aunt after not seeing them for many years. I had no intention of coming back to visit, and I counted down the days until I could leave. My residence there lasted only a year, which was enough to last me a lifetime.

El Paso had freezing cold winters and drenching hot summers. Some days got dangerously hot to the point that we couldn't go outside. From the moment of our arrival, I knew that this city wasn't going to provide me with an opportunity to succeed. A sign of hope for a progressing and promising future was nowhere in sight. Going to school was my mission, but it wasn't a realistic option for me since I had to work to make a living in Texas. Every time someone asks me about how I filled my days while in El Paso, my answer always surprises them; I continued my learning of the German language because after seeing no opportunity to get an education, I was planning towards moving back and pursuing an education there. I did not want to forget any part of the language I had learned thus far, so I asked my friends from Germany to send me books from which to study. They thought I was losing my mind when I would ask them for the study materials. They would raise the question, "She's lucky enough to be in America. Why would she possibly want to excel in the German language?"

I praise God for his wisdom during the panning out of my life, which took many unexpected turns, but nonetheless, ended up as a blessing. In God's will, there was an alternative. I could relocate to the Golden State, otherwise known as California. After living with my brother and his family for about a year, we said our farewells and left for Los Angeles, California. This was the city that allowed me to establish my permanent home, my final destination—a place which I wouldn't exchange for any other place in the world.

Happy to finally settle in a city where I felt a sense of belonging, I was excited about the abundance of opportunities I had with doors left wide open. I started my first job in LA just within three weeks upon our arrival. Working ten hours a day in a car wash gift shop was not easy, but not impossible for a young girl dedicated to turning her life into something extraordinary. The car wash owner's wife was one of our old neighbors back in Iran and was even acquainted with my mother many years ago. They offered me a job for the sake of respect for my mother because they knew her as a highly respectable individual. My job there was to handle the cash register. At times there were over three to four thousand dollars in hard cash in those cash registers. My training was only two hours of using the cash register, and just like that, I became responsible for the money that was flowing in and out of the store.

At the time, the minimum wage was $3.35. But, the owners agreed to pay me $3.75 because they knew my family. Through long tiring hours of working at the shop and extra pay through overtime, I managed to earn $700 every month. My rent was $400, so I was left with $300 to spend however I pleased, including spending on necessities, of course. It was a dream of mine to lease a Toyota MR2 sports car. Yup, that was the car of the year, and I fell in love with it. The first time I saw it was when one of my male friends bought one and drove it over to show me. Shortly after this, he ended up asking me to be his girlfriend. Despite falling for his car, I had definitely not fallen for him, so my answer was a definite no. My refusal to date him crushed whatever ego he possessed, and I knew this because he started driving by my apartment building with a different girl every time to show off the car and the unfortunate girl who was riding shotgun.

We had a window opening on Central Avenue's busy street in Glendale, where we resided, so our apartment was easy to spot. The MR2 guy became my first ever stalker. He knew what time I was getting home for work and would drive up and down our street to get my attention. Little did he know I was more interested in seeing his car than him. I loved watching the scene of that beautiful sports car racing along our street, but at the same time pretending he wasn't the one driving it. The car absolutely took my breath away. "I will buy an MR2 someday," I thought to myself. I was working in the gift shop for about 6-7 months and knew the regular clients by their first names. One hot and busy Saturday afternoon, I had been working for eight hours, feeling more exhausted than usual. We opened the store as early as 7 am so I had been on my feet for a long while. A tall man wearing prescription glasses with a very serious but well-mannered demeanor approached me. He asked me if I was interested in potentially making more money by becoming a model. My height was 5'7", and weighing 118 pounds at the time, this offer didn't seem too farfetched. He handed me his business card containing his information while asking me what my current paycheck looked like knowing that it probably wasn't much. After I told him I made minimum wage, he assured me he could help me make at least a hundred times more than that, with much less effort.

I believe that things always happen for a reason. At that moment, a regular customer was standing close enough to passively hear our conversation. He was my favorite one, an older guy in his sixties named Andrew. Sadly, no matter how hard I try, I'm not able to remember his last name. So we're going to leave his name as Andrew. After the modeling recruiter left, Andrew walked up to me and asked me to be very careful if I did decide to take him up on his offer and never agree to meet him anywhere discreet. Andrew was at the car wash often, so we had built a friendship. He was a very wise gentleman, so engaging in conversations with him was an enjoyable pastime making my boring job a little less tedious. He spoke very softly, and every word was timely said, knowing that my English was a work in progress. It was always a pleasant surprise when he came in for a car wash.

A week had gone by, and I decided to call the modeling recruiter who had given me his business card. We agreed to meet on a Monday morning, which was my day off. Thinking of Andrew's advice, I asked my friend to accompany me when we met in his office. Walking into his office with one of my close girlfriends by my side wasn't something the recruiter expected, judging from the change in his behavior. It was becoming clearer throughout our encounter that he thought I was another naive girl from a foreign country speaking broken English.

It was hard to believe he didn't consciously perceive the immorality in his intention. After giving my friend and me a few strange looks, he then asked me to follow him to his office, but my friend had to wait in the reception area. It was a moderately big office, but there was no secretary or employee in sight. Perhaps the office was closed on Mondays? I couldn't put my finger on what was making this whole experience feel so strange, but I knew something wasn't right.

In his office, he grabbed a ruler and started to measure various parts of my body. I was beginning to feel very uncomfortable because the whole process was feeling more demeaning as time progressed. He was moving the ruler up and down toward my upper legs. I felt the ruler inch closer to my privates. That's when he crossed the line and I immediately made him stop. Being confused and embarrassed, not knowing if what I had done was warranted, I called my friend for help. She made it to the office where I was, and we made our way out. My friend said she was so startled when I yelled her name that she ran towards the exit rather than coming to my rescue. The recruiter was annoyed and acted like something was wrong with me, stating that he was only doing his job. Whether or not this was actually a part of the modeling process, I wasn't up for it. I didn't need a job that made me feel like I didn't have a say in what parts of my body could be touched. I can not allow a stranger to freely touch my body as if it is theirs to feel.

The following week Andrew came to the shop while I was at work and could not wait to hear about my meeting with the modeling agent. He listened to my horrible experience and let me confide in him, for which I was grateful. The first thing that left his mouth was," Violet, you're young and bright. Stop wasting your time. You need an education here to better your life and shouldn't waste time in the process." He proceeded to offer me a job at the company he worked for. I appreciated his excellent advice and offer, but I needed time to adjust to my new lifestyle and couldn't risk trying to work somewhere else. There was still a war going on in our country Iran. My mother could not help us financially because transferring money was out of the question. Regardless of whether she could send money, the last thing I wanted was to be a burden for my mother, expecting her to pay for my living expenses. I was already 21 years old, and my ego never enabled me to accept my mother's financial assistance. I was too independent to accept money, even from my own mother.

Andrew was persistent in convincing me to quit my job to come and work for the company at which he was employed. It was a reputable insurance company, but I had moved to the city only a few months prior, and I needed more time to excel in my English before holding an office job. I had no experience in an office. Nonetheless, I applied for the job knowing I was underqualified, which still surprises me. I can still remember the day I walked to the Coastal Insurance Company and asked for a man named Andrew. Knowing that I finally applied for the job, Andrew told me prior to my arrival to go to the main receptionist and ask for him. The receptionist questioned me with her snarky attitude, "You're here to see Andrew?" "Yes, he's expecting me," I responded, feeling uncertain at this point about what position Andrew held at this large company.

I was surprised as I was escorted to his office to see him sitting behind a huge beautiful mahogany desk. After being alone with him in his office, I said, "Andrew, who are you?" My face looked so innocent and shocked. Andrew found it humorous and started laughing. He said he was the Vice President of the company and would like to hire me as his secretary's assistant. His secretary needed assistance, and he said I was the perfect fit. Andrew insisted that I was full of potential, and a car wash gift shop wasn't a place for a young girl to begin establishing a career. I wanted to accept his offer very badly, but I doubted my capability. It would be a big task working as an assistant secretary with no prior experience or language proficiency. He knew very well where I stood and was still willing to give me a chance.

People walk into our lives at various stages, and some of those people leave an imprint in our hearts forever. They leave us with memories that will never fade away, always staying fresh in our hearts as well as our minds. Andrew was a Cuban who immigrated to the United States, which made him understand the obstacles immigrants face upon arrival to a new country. Not only did he understand, but he was empathetic and really tried to leave a positive impact on the world. Andrew proved to me that there are men out there who are kind enough to use their privilege to help people when given a chance with no ulterior motive. He was like a saint and would help everyone in any way that he could, even at work.

That insurance company ended up being the foundation of my work experience in the U.S. It was very challenging working at a position for which I had no background knowledge, but Andrew was always very patient during my learning process. He believed in my abilities, so it was my goal never to let him down. I was so grateful for that car wash gift shop because if it weren't for my job there, I would have never met Andrew, who gave me the opportunity to build my career. He entered my life and made a lasting mark that was more than just opening the door to wonderful work experience. Andrew served as my mentor for the longest time during my employment there, always giving me wise yet humble advice on anything you could think of. He even introduced me to Cuban food, something I had never had the pleasure of coming across in my country.

Unfortunately, my time working at this insurance company was short-lived. Not too long after I began my employment there, the company went bankrupt and was closed down. I was upset that the job I loved and just got hired for no longer existed, but I was grateful that I got to experience working there even for the few months that I did. I was also very thankful to be able to add this position to my resume, considering the company was one of many prestigious companies at the time. After gaining some experience through my first insurance job, I started working for another insurance company with my title as "data entry personnel." Before resigning, my final title was a "recovery analyst," which took about ten years of working to acquire.

I was in a stable place at my new insurance job, but my hunger for knowledge was yet to be satiated. I began taking college courses at the local community college, and simultaneously taking insurance courses paid for by the company for which I was working. Every time I passed a course and obtained a completion certificate, I would earn a company bonus. Of course, this motivated me to take more of these courses, in the hope of opening my own insurance agency someday. This seemed like a win-win situation. Although I was making a livable income from the insurance company, I was reluctant to settle for the bare minimum. I had obtained a certificate to become a travel agent at nights after my day job and was selling destinations. Keeping my morning job was a must for me since I really needed the flexible hours. I was attending school several nights out of the week part-time and always looking for new certifications for which to qualify. I needed to be able to work only in the mornings and have the ability to switch around my schedule in case I was taking on a new job or project.

Moving to America, I could spend only so much money on a car, which limited my options, considering I had my eyes on flashy sports cars. I ensured a stable income source and bought my first car, which was as close I could get to what I was looking for. It was a white dodge colt. It wasn't the MR2 like the one my friend had, but it still did well for me. It allowed me to gain a sense of independence as a young working woman in America, and I was grateful. However, I went to work everyday knowing that with every paycheck I was getting closer to my dream car. It was an excellent long term goal I had set for myself, and it made me work a bit harder. Some time had passed, and I finally saved enough to get my hands on my Toyota MR2. I loved that car so much that just being inside of it put me in the best mood. Not only did I love the car for its appearance and fast, sporty drive, but I loved that I had worked hard for months to possess it, and it was finally mine. Unfortunately, my adventure with this car came to an end abruptly after getting into a terrible freeway accident. It was a rainy day, and I was on my way to work when I got rear-ended so badly, that the impact sent my car spinning into the middle of oncoming traffic. I vowed to myself that I would never drive a sports car ever again.

We can plan our futures as much as we please, but nothing can interfere with the plan that God has in store for us. After familiarizing myself with the working world in America, the next upcoming vision I had for myself was to open my own insurance agency. My first office job working for Andrew was such a pleasant memory that the thought of having my own insurance company seemed like a real dream job. My self-employment goal pushed me toward obtaining the necessary certificates and licenses for many years so I could improve my knowledge in my chosen field. I really wanted to settle down and have a business of my own, to feel like I was truly making a lasting footprint in my name.

When I met my husband, I was in no rush to start a family. The concept of marriage wasn't something I thought about often, nor was it something I anticipated. I never thought of it as my ideal situation because I always looked at marriage like a birdcage—two birds coexisting in one cage, possibly even happier together, but yet struggling to fly free. I had compared myself to birds all my life. People have certain similarities to birds, one of the most important being that we were meant to fly and thrive without the confinement of boundaries or cages. We were meant to constantly improve our lives and aim for self-growth, and that was a sense of flying free. No matter how fancy or appealing the cage may appear, flying was always my instinct. I thought this was always going to be how I viewed marriage, but someone special entered my life who changed my perspective forever.

I met my husband at a social event which I attended with my close friends. I finally met the one who was so different from all of the others that he changed how I thought about men. Someone with whom I could trust and share my life with. A person who would be the perfect father figure for my future children. I knew I could see his love for children every time he would encounter my niece, who was only two years old at the time. He was so nurturing and would look after her with the same care as a father would with his own child. He had this caring and protective nature that was very easy to notice even upon the first time meeting him.

After meeting my husband and reconstructing my thoughts on marriage, we decided it was time to get married. Once again, nothing comes easy for me. During that sensitive time in my life, I suffered from severe aches and pains in my abdomen. My menstrual cycles substantially worsened and the pain became intolerable. The cause of this was left undiagnosed by my doctors and was a mystery to me. After enduring a few long months of painful days and excruciating nights, a revelation was finally made by one very wise doctor who was able to make a definite diagnosis. I had an ovarian tumor and had to undergo surgery to determine if it was cancerous or not. The doctor could not give me any form of reassurance as to whether or not the tumor had damaged my reproductive system. I could never bear a child if the tumor were cancerous or if it was sitting on my ovaries. I was heartbroken from this awful news because it placed me in another setback rather than in a progression. This diagnosis put a significant damper on my mood because it was in the midst of finally talking about starting a family.

Finally, deciding that marriage and creating a family was something that I now wanted and envisioned, I knew that I had to let go of this now established fantasy. I could not go on with the relationship with my soon to be fiance because it was not fair to him. He was a man who loved children and wanted some of his own. My condition could potentially deprive him of that. I decided to end my relationship. My husband's persistence didn't allow him to give up on the idea of the family that we both wanted. Once again, God answered my prayers. Not only was the tumor not cancerous, but it didn't even damage any part of my ovaries. According to the doctor, It was God's will for me to survive, given the size of the tumor; it was one pound. I got rid of the tumor and cancer scare, but medical students in a research facility somewhere in America gained a massive tumor to study.

I faced all of my friends and family the moment after I said, "I do," to my husband at the altar and saw about two hundred butterflies released into the sunset. It was a breathtaking sight to see. My favorite living creature has always been a butterfly. Not just because I admire their graceful and unique beauty, but because I see a piece of myself in every butterfly. Butterflies fly freely in their habitats, and I believe that I have been navigating with a sense of freedom throughout my life. I do not let things hold me back from what I truly want; ultimately, my destiny.

Knowing my appreciation for butterflies, my oldest sister had ordered a couple hundred butterflies kept in tiny boxes for my wedding. One small enclosed package caging a beautiful live butterfly was handed to each wedding guest. This was such a special addition to my wedding because, for me, it was a representation of my soul breaking free from all that was holding me back from marriage. It was a reminder that I was always going to be that free-flying butterfly. My wedding ceremony was in the outdoor poolside area of the Marriott Hotel. I had always wanted to have an outdoor ceremony instead of an indoor church service. Despite my preference, I still arranged for a priest to come to our party to bless our wedding because of my strong Christian beliefs. Now, I look back and wonder if I had any plan B, should rain be in the forecast for the Saturday of October 2003. Mother nature was on our side, and we ended with a beautiful wedding surrounded by love from our friends and families.

Every pregnancy is a miracle, but the news of mine gave my husband and me so much more to be grateful for. Especially the terrible obstacle I had just overcome regarding my reproductive organs only fifty days before our child's conception. I had experienced many things in my life, but motherhood was incomparable. It is a heavenly feeling of a completely different nature. The bliss that arises from knowing that you are carrying another life in you cannot be mimicked. Whatever title I had before having my children: travel agent, real estate agent, or insurance broker, it did not define me. One very important title I gained after giving birth to my firstborn, which I can confidently say, defines me: mother. I am my children's mom. I quit my jobs and my endless chase for an even more elite position, and if I had to sacrifice it again to raise my children, I would. I do not regret my decision because being a mother is the most priceless title I could have ever obtained.

Chapter Eight

BELONGING

My dream of moving to America was finally a reality, and with this new life of mine, my sense of belonging increased. I was always very curious about sociology, so I did my own personal study of people throughout my life. The people I focused on were the group that I identify with most. These are Iranian Armenian people who have experienced many cultural and national similarities as me. I have always been fascinated by how we fit into a Muslim country and culture so different from ours. With this notion, I was beginning to pay close attention to myself in relation to society, as an attempt to find my place. Upon moving to several countries, I compared myself to various cities in all the different countries in which I had lived.

Thinking about myself in relation to the few countries I had lived in, I was struck with a realization not many would attempt to see. Through self-reflection, I realized the concept of belonging, in a much bigger picture, and in a way that I had never considered before. Through my unique perspective, I came to understand that Armenian people from Iran never really belonged to solely one country. I am talking about the Armenians who have lived in Iran for centuries, like my family. Iran is all that we have known all of our lives, but we never quite fit in with the majority population since we were a minority group amongst the Iranians. We were well respected, and we got along with the Iranians, but we were still Armenian.

In Iran, Armenians had just as much opportunity as Iranians to live a prosperous life. They were provided the opportunity to get an education as well as exercise the same rights. However, there were some limitations for Armenians and their ability to uphold government-appointed positions and military positions. We were still limited in our involvement with the Iranian government. Armenians were still allowed to join the military and in fact, legally had to participate if they got drafted. During the Revolution, many Armenian men fled the country to avoid being drafted into the war. Being allowed to join the military meant they could only get so far up in rank. Armenian men were never allowed to hold a position as an influential military leader due to being minorities.

Armenians who live in Iran are proud of their nationality and the array of cultural assimilations that come with living there. However, due to the great pride we share as Armenians for our ethnic background, we find ourselves at odds when it comes time to accept a country other than Armenia as our origin. Despite living in Iran for hundreds of years, the Armenian people and our ancestors consider themselves Armenian before anything else. This explains why we have been reluctant to completely assimilate to the Iranian people. Our ability to preserve our ethnic identity has allowed us to maintain our Armenian heritage as well as simultaneously embracing our Iranian nationality.

We were amongst the small minority of Christians to share a country strongly dominated by Islamic rule. Armenians typically lean towards a more conservative style, but nowhere as stern as Iran's traditional ideals. In Armenian households, women had a greater sense of independence and equality than is traditionally seen in the Iranian lifestyle. For example, we did not always maintain the belief that the man accompanying a woman in the street necessarily had to be her husband or significant other. We also did not believe that women had to cover up their hair or their bodies. These Iranian laws were set by the strong Islamic government that came into power after The Shah of Iran.

One question that might arise as you read this is why Armenian people in Iran don't just find their way back to Armenia. That is their home, after all. This is where it's a bit complicated. Armenians have a diaspora placing them in different regions other than their homeland, the country of Armenia. Amongst these include countries such as Iran, Lebanon, Russia, and the homeland of

Armenia. The origin of the Armenian people is in the small country of Armenia. The diaspora, which places Armenians in different countries, creates certain differences amongst these people living in other countries. One difference is that the language slightly varies depending on the country in which you reside. The main dialects are split into two; the Eastern and the Western.

Although Iranian Armenians and Armenians from Armenia do share the common dialect of speaking Eastern Armenian, there is still hesitation about their merging. The two groups of Armenians greatly respect one another, but the difference of nationality makes it hard for Iranian Armenians to consider Armenia their first home. Iran is all that we have known, and it has been like that for hundreds of years. Armenia is still our homeland, but at the same time, so is Iran. Adapting to Iranian culture and embracing its cultural traditions allowed us to consider it home, but at the same time, we are not Persians. Never being attached physically to our homeland of Armenia also makes it hard to call it our only home.

My short move to Germany also opened my eyes to this notion as well. Of course, I was too busy focusing on this new transition rather than trying to confirm or deny anything involving the social theory I was conjuring up in my mind. I took a short break from thinking about my true sense of belonging, ironically, because I was subconsciously trying to fit in. Even though I wasn't intending to stay there for a long time, it was instinctual to try my best to conform to Germany's norms. These included culture, how I spent my hours in the day, and my style. I was taking a break from thinking about it so much because I was living it. We are all trying to fit in somehow, which is another aspect that involves our sense of belonging.

Reflecting back on my life in Germany gives me even more insight into my understanding of nationality. Maybe it was because Iran had always been my home, but a small part of me was still in search of another place. Iran was and will forever be my home, but as much as I consider it my home, I am still Armenian by blood. I did not expect to make Germany my home as I knew that I wouldn't be living there forever. My stay was temporary, but my readiness to adapt to another country's customs was natural to me.

My move to America really confirmed the belief I had regarding the Iranian Armenian peoples' reluctance to fit in completely in one country. But in a way, that was a shocking new truth. After moving to the States, I knew that this was a permanent transition. If there was any time that I had to conform to culture and lifestyle it had to have been then. Moving to a country that is practically a polar opposite in comparison to your hometown is not easy, to say the least. America and Iran are vastly different countries dissimilar in respects that must go uncounted because of their abundance. The cultural traditions that we had in Iran were nowhere to be seen in America, and America's traditions were unfamiliar to me.

America was drastically different from Iran in almost

every way imaginable. The freedom promoted in America was not readily available in Iran due to the government enforcement of a more restrictive lifestyle. The lifestyle in America was drastically different from that in Iran, mainly in aspects of modesty. Women specifically were just as free as men to wear whatever they pleased and roam in the street with whomever they wanted. As new and exciting as it was, it was such a new lifestyle change for me.

I went from covering up my hair in Iran to coming to America where I was almost praised for showing off my freshly done-up hair. In Iran you could get in serious trouble if your hijab wasn't securely placed, and your hair was visible to the naked eye. When you were caught for disobeying the law, it was also suggested that you not talk back to the police because that would result in a greater consequence, including possible jail time. It was amazing to me that I now lived in a country where the law promoted freedom of speech and the attire that you chose was your business only. I would see women half-clothed in the street living their daily life, and it was just as shocking as it was refreshing.

I was used to my Armenian lifestyle, living all those years within the constraints of an Islamic nation, now finding myself living in the land of the free—America. I was never as conservative as my Armenian peers and definitely not as conservative as the way Islamic life encourages. This was what made me so fascinated by this country. A place where everyone is accepted and able to freely practice any religion and believe whatever they want to about this world we share. This country took me in with open arms and allowed me to be whoever I wanted and allowed me to live how I wanted without limitations.

Despite my having to become accustomed to the many changes, I was trying my best. I still wanted to do all I could to fit into this new country I was calling my home because that is exactly what it was becoming. I was trying to adapt to the working life at such a young age while keeping up with the young party scene California had to offer. In my early twenties, there were many changes to get used to, including anything from the way that I had to dress, to how I had to speak. By doing so however, I was still holding on tightly to my Iranian Armenian values.

It is alright to consider yourself belonging to not just one country, but more. I was succeeding at my jobs, getting used to the culture, and learning American-style etiquette. Adapting was not easy, but I was coming closer each and every day. Until this day I have grown to realize that it is not essential to try and belong solely to one country. It is essential to belong wherever you believe your home to be. This being said, America had become my home.

My experience in Iran and different countries, with one of them being my new home, has made me realize how unique it was to be an Iranian Armenian becoming an American as well. I am so proud to come from where

I do and be who I am as an Armenian woman, but I acknowledge that we Iranian Armenians do not belong to just one place. We do not view one single country as our homeland. I am Armenian, but Iran is closer to home for me because that is where I was born and where I grew up. This is my interpretation of it because I know there are so many ways people comprehend their sense of national belonging.

My analysis has led me to an understanding most people probably don't come to. It is the understanding that Iranian Armenian people have more than one place with which to associate. I loved my home in Iran, and being Armenian. I loved my short time in Germany, and finally, establishing my permanent place as an American. I proudly call myself an American because I consider myself just as American as anybody else. My childhood years and my traditions belong to Iran, my heritage and culture are Armenian, and a part of who I am is a proud American. I have lived over half of my life here, and I truly believe that this country has become my home. I belong to more than one nation, and that is what makes Iranian-Armenian Americans like me, as well as myself, special.

If one belongs to more than one country, then in theory it makes for belonging to more than one country. I always like to justify the world around me and my relation to it which is what led me to even think about my place in the countries I called home. The Armenian blood running through my veins, the Iranian culture and life in which I was raised, and being an American for my adult life until the present, makes my sense of belonging a combination rather than all or nothing.

Thinking about the concept of belonging to more than one place wasn't something that I saw as a bad thing. It was just something that I noticed in people who shared my same experience. It got easier to notice as years went by because I experienced more of this world, with my perspective being the guide. The Armenian culture, the values I learned in Iran, and my Westernized mentality being an American were all things that made me different in a positive way. I always noticed how I was too Armenian for Iran, not Armenian enough for Armenia, and too ethnic to be a real American. But all in all, I was an embodiment of all these countries.

Upholding my belief that I am just as American as the next person and that I am proud to belong to a country so full of opportunity, I pass down my way of thinking. I have raised my children as proud Americans, as well as upholding Persian and Armenian values. My children grew up embracing their Persian and Armenian heritage but considering themselves American. They were born here, so their situation was slightly different than mine because being born in the States automatically made you a little more American by title. Despite still having ethnic values, I instilled confidence in my children that this was their country, and their aspirations could be anything, even if that meant running for the presidency.

Everyone has their own justification for how they fit

into the world around them, and this is mine. I believe that as an Iranian- Armenian American, I do not belong to only one country, and that is what makes my experience mine. This is my concept of how I fit into the world around me, and the fact that it is so special makes it beautiful. If everything were interpreted the same way by everyone in this world, we would all be living the same life.

Seeing the diversity in all the cultures an Iranian-Armenian American belongs to makes me believe that it is in fact, an extraordinary thing to belong to more than one place. Every country has its own beautiful traditions and norms set for living, and not being from just one country allows for embracing all of them. I am grateful to come from more than one place and belong to more than one country. I am an Armenian from Iran, who is also an American.

Chapter Nine

MAMMOGRAM

When I was scheduled for my first mammogram, I was not worried, nor did I have any anxiety over the screening. Unlike my friends who feared going through their first mammogram, I was quite courageous when it came to things like this. They worried about the process itself, but most importantly, the results. Convinced that breast cancer is mostly linked to inherited genes and being fairly common amongst women, most of my friends had a family member who had it. "This isn't the case for me, so I have nothing to worry about," I always thought to myself. I knew of no one in my immediate family or amongst my relatives that had been diagnosed or battled breast cancer. Considering that I came from a big family and still have no known relatives diagnosed with any form of cancer, it made me feel confident.

The day came for my mammogram, and I will have

to admit it was somewhat uncomfortable and even a bit painful. The pain felt more like pressure that was so strong it was hard to differentiate from pain. After my mammogram was over and sent to the radiologist for evaluation, I got a call shortly after. The doctor told me that since my breasts are so dense, I am at a higher risk of developing breast cancer. He stressed the importance of never failing to miss any of my routine and annual mammograms. I took his advice very seriously and continued to monitor myself and had routine mammograms every 8 to 9 months. It was around the fourth or the fifth mammogram, one late evening I received a call from Cedars Sinai Hospital regarding suspicious findings. They wanted me to go back for a more complete diagnostic image. Surprisingly, not even that scared me. They were going to have to do better than that, and they did.

After the diagnostic mammogram, I was escorted to the doctor's office, where I was told the mammogram showed some microcalcifications in both of my breasts. He explained that they are small calcium deposits that are usually not a result of cancer, but on my imaging, they appeared in specific patterns and were clustered together. He said that it is a possibility that it is a sign of precancerous cells. Seeing that I became increasingly nervous, he added that his wife and daughter had the same type of calcifications and had lumpectomies due to each occurrence.

However, my tumors were in very deep tissue and needed surgical biopsies instead of standard ones. The doctor referred me to several general surgeons. I conducted research on five different surgeons that were referred to me. I even interviewed three of them in person until I felt comfortable with making a decision. A doctor's credentials were essential to me because they reflected the success, he or she had curing their patients. The doctor I chose was knowledgeable, attentive, mature, skillful, a great listener, and he had over 30 years of experience. He had done several thousand surgeries in the years he had been practicing, and he was the one I trusted to help get me out of this state in my life.

It was already December, and I put my Christmas tree up earlier than usual that year as my way of wishing nothing but good health to my family and myself. A week after the biopsy surgery, my surgeon called me at home and gave me the good news. It was the evening of December 22nd, just a day and a half before Christmas Eve. The biopsy results showed that the calcifications they detected were DCIS (ductal carcinoma in situ). The good news to this was that the margins and all the surrounding tissues were clear. That meant there was no unhealthy tissue left in either one of my breasts. Regardless of my current good health, I was required to follow up with a mammogram every three months for the next year and every six months after that for added precaution.

They always say life is all about making choices. Life is the byproduct of those choices. I agree. My choice to undergo a double mastectomy and reconstruction surgery was an intensely personal and difficult decision. Unfortunately, we do not have the luxury to determine the severity of an illness when it comes into our lives. Despite a clear diagnostic mammogram and a needle biopsy conducted three months before my surgery, showing no signs of a vicious cancerous tumor, I was still a victim. I had an option to undergo a double mastectomy, so I decided to do that rather than ending up in a situation with no more room for choices. With that said, I am not trying to instill fear in my reader's mind, but instead, I hope that my experience and the choices I made as a response to them can ignite questions and maybe even lead one to making a decision that could end up sparing their life.

When I decided to treat ductal carcinoma in situ (DCIS) with the most aggressive method - bilateral mastectomy – at that time, no hospital or doctors treated their DCIS patients with this method. For starters, insurance companies did not see the surgery as a necessary treatment option. Second, the surgery would be considered an elective one rather than needed. When I discussed my thoughts with my oncologist and the surgeon, they were both strongly against my decision. DCIS back in those years was referred to as stage 0 breast cancer. It was considered a precancerous condition, which is not the case today. Doctors' visions on treatments regarding this diagnosis have shifted gears immensely, making the approval of a bilateral mastectomy very unlikely. Despite what I had to go through; I still thank God for the timing of my misfortune.

My last mammogram in October 2012 showed no evidence of any cancer, had a clear image, and my BRCA testing was negative. The BRCA gene test is a blood test done to determine if you have changes (mutations) in your DNA that increase the risk of breast cancer. People who inherit mutations in these genes are at higher risk of developing breast cancer and ovarian cancer than those who do not. My doctors offered me different treatment alternatives. But I felt that undergoing a double mastectomy was the only chance of my survival.

My surgery was scheduled for February 13, 2013. More people than not, maintain the belief that the number 13 symbolizes bad luck. It was an early winter morning when I lifted my noticeably heavy eyelids, emerging back to consciousness from an operation performed just hours ago. I was still coming out of the effects of the anesthesia, which made me very groggy, leaving me scattered in my own thoughts. I was dazed and confused with the heaviest pressure on my chest I had ever felt, making me wonder where I was. It was past midnight when they transitioned me from the recovery room to a more private room, laying me down. It was a surprisingly spacious room with a sitting area looking much nicer than your typical hospital room.

It wasn't until I saw a glimpse of the Star of David on top of the Cedars Sinai Hospital from my window, did I realize my current situation. With a smile of victory and pride, I thought to myself, "You kicked cancer goodbye before it grew the chance of harming you and your family." I said my prayers and shared my gratitude while looking up to the Star of David. I was told that the hospital where I was, was representative of Jewish values, which consisted of care for all people, and active contribution to a better world for all. To me, the star of David still maintains a valuable religious meaning despite belonging to a different religion. The star's presence gave me a sense of peace and confidence. "You did it," I told myself. You took matters into your own hands and made a decision that could have been regretted if it wasn't made. "It's over!" I said as my final thought. Now I can tell my children that they don't have to worry about losing their momma to breast cancer.

I felt empowered and very proud of myself for making a decision that was going to make my life great. Even though my doctors typically weren't advocates of such an aggressive way of handling ductal carcinoma in situ (DCIS), believing that I should have considered alternatives, I was content. When I showed up at the hospital on the day of my surgery, the plastic surgeon said to me, "I honestly thought you wouldn't show up for your procedure today." He said many women cancel their surgery at the last minute due to hesitation from such a big decision. He thought I would not stick to my decision since my condition was not life-threatening enough to leave me without a choice.

I couldn't sleep the night of the surgery and was

worried about my surgery and wondering if I was making the right decision. Little did my surgeon know that the night before, I did think about calling off the surgery altogether. However, I had one of those feelings again that inched me closer to one decision rather than the other making me keep the plan intact. It was three in the morning when I walked into my husband's office at our home. I knew he was up working. As I opened the door that morning, my eye caught the article he was reading. He was researching mastectomies, trying to learn about the potential side effects. He closed the tab on his computer immediately after he noticed me entering his office. Just by looking at my face, he could tell that I was having second thoughts about the surgery. He asked me if I was worried. My answer was, "No, that is your job. You worry enough for the both of us." I just wanted reassurance from him that this was the right thing to do, but when I asked him, he said, "Please do not ask me to tell you what to do. It's your body, it's a decision only you can make, and I respect that."

I was discharged three days after my surgery. I missed my children, and all I wanted was to recover in the comfort of my home with my family around me. The doctors suggested extending my stay in the hospital because it was a really invasive procedure. My mastectomy was followed by reconstruction simultaneously, which was why I had drains near my breasts. However, since I had no complications, I was able to go home with the drains inserted, of course. I was given instructions on caring for the drains before I left the hospital. The fluid had to be emptied from the detachable drain bulb a few times a day before they were removed during the first office visit after the surgery.

When my surgeon called me at home and asked if I had received the biopsy results yet, I sensed that the streak of bad news wasn't over yet. He asked me if I wanted to hear the good news or the bad news first. I am the type to look at life like a cup half full, so of course, I chose to hear the good news first. Once he started by telling me he was glad that I went through the procedure, I knew there would be some bad news to follow.

He continued saying that the tissue biopsies' results showed that I had a few DCIS in my right breast, and in the left, there was evidence of tiny invasive cancerous cells. The word "invasive" sounded scary and harsh to my ears because of all of the pain that word has caused me in the past. It means that the cancer had invaded or spread to the surrounding breast tissues. "It was a wise decision to follow through with the mastectomy even with a clear mammogram and negative BRCA," he said. What is next, I thought to myself after hanging up the phone. Since my surgery was considered a preventive procedure and no lymph nodes were removed during the operation, a lymph node biopsy was necessary. This was necessary to determine whether the cancer had spread, giving the doctors more insight to determine the stage and the corresponding treatment.

I Immediately requested another surgery to be scheduled for the removal of a few lymph nodes. It was important to me to find out whether any of the nodes carried those vicious cancer cells. Knowing that my request for a double mastectomy worked out in my favor, the doctors did not try to dissuade me this time around. Just three weeks later, I was back in the operating room for yet another surgery. The surgery was successful, and the cancer had not dispersed through the lymphatic system. Although I was in the clear, I was prescribed medication for 5 to 7 years as a preventative measure to demolish any microscopic cancer cells that might still be lingering. When I look back on my experience, I am overflowed with relief and gratitude to know that my drastic decisions served a purpose.

This entire experience was a reminder never to take the power of prayer lightly and to be careful what we request from God. I was always taught in church to be specific with what we are asking from God, and this is an example of why that can be problematic. A direct answer to prayer was not a good thing in my case since these results just made my situation even more difficult. While I repeatedly prayed for having a clear mammogram and not showing any signs of tumor, every time I underwent the mammogram screening, God answered my prayers with precisely the way I pleaded. My prayers were technically granted, but not in the way that I had hoped.

There are many biblical examples where God eventually grants his people's persistent yet imprudent prayers, including mine. What this taught me was that although my prayer was granted in such an ironic way, it was not fully lost in translation. The ultimate prayer I wished to have granted was to be healthy, and God did, in fact, bless me in that way. We have to maintain the hope that the end goal of our prayers will eventually be answered in significant ways. God may have a different path or some creative means of accomplishing his will in our lives, and it is much more complex than a simple prayer and answer. Feeling almost like I was given a second chance at life; I couldn't help but feel like it was the work of God that spared my life. But how would I figure out if that's what it was? Maybe I was just making decisions because of influences in my life, or perhaps it was God's force that was the drive behind the choices I made. My choice was to pray to God for my health and have the strength to have an operation that could potentially saved my life. Some questions will never get answers, but I'm just hoping my words spark a decision or a create hope in someone that may result in their life being spared as my life was.

Recovery from the surgery took some time, and luckily, I had a caring and loving family helping me when I needed to do daily tasks. And thankful for the access to childcare since my older son was nine and the little one only three years of age. As my body was healing and adjusting itself to the surgery's effects over several months, my husband made sure the process was as comfortable as possible. We went on many trips. The one to Florida was just a month after the surgery. The surgery was in February, and we were out and about in March. It was Spring Break, and the kids were home from school, which meant it was time for our regular spring vacation. It's very common for the families in the school community to go on trips every time there is a long break. Since this was something we always did as well, I did not want my children to feel anything different from the previous years.

I remember our trip to Florida that Spring very well. I was feeling so good that I had forgotten that I had undergone surgery not too long ago. I attempted to carry my own luggage when all of a sudden, my arms felt numb, making me drop everything, causing me to fall to the ground alongside them. Not used to seeing their mom tumble over like that, my kids' expressions looked as if they were watching a scene from a horror movie. Despite the embarrassment and the pain I felt, I burst out laughing, which ended up being contagious, leaving us laughing at what just happened. They walked over and helped me up, and we continued making our way through the airport. It was vital for me to make sure that this vacation happened because I wanted everything to be normal again after such a significant change in my life. Seeing my children having fun and making new memories fueled our return to normalcy, and I couldn't have been happier.

As my nerves regrew in my breasts, I felt a weird crawling and itching sensation on my chest, making it very sensitive to touch. It ended up going away on its own, but for almost two years I was unable to swim using my arms. The muscles of my chest wall did not want to cooperate with me every time I tried to swim. This was disheartening because swimming is one of my favorite activities. I was getting physical therapy three times a week, and it did not seem to help much. This only discouraged me more, but did not make me lose hope.

I am not a quitter when I determine to reach a goal and being able to swim again was a new goal for me. I continued my therapy, followed the doctor's orders, and kept a positive mindset. It was the summer of 2015 when I started to swim again, just like nothing had ever happened. During the whole experience, I vowed to myself to turn my journey and what I had lived through into something useful for myself and others. The takeaway from this is never to lose hope or take no for an answer, even when the odds are against you.

Cancer transformed my self-perception and how I analyzed life as a whole. It also taught me to appreciate and be grateful for the things I have in my life. I learned that having a healthy and positive outlook was much more worthwhile than self-pity. I started to smile more often and endure any pain or hardship with grace and optimism. In the end, cancer taught me that I am stronger than I thought I was. I am even getting more robust with my thought processes, continually reminding myself that life is too short to live through fear and doubt. With this new mindset, I am living my life to the fullest. I have always loved traveling, but now my family and I travel the world for different purposes. We are making lasting memories together as a family. I want my children to remember me in every location on Earth when they travel in the future with their own families—when I am no longer with them. I thank God for granting me more time with my children, and I want to make the rest of my time on Earth, one that will be remembered.

I have lost many friends and acquaintances to breast cancer, and it raised the question, "why them?" After my personal experience, that question turned into, "why me?" "Why did this have to happen to me?" I think about the heartfelt stories of people I know who lost their lives. I believe I was spared because this entire experience was meant as an opportunity and outlet for me to transfer this newfound energy and hunger for life towards something beneficial for others wearing the same shoes I once wore.

One of my life's main goals is to help less fortunate individuals receive treatment for their breast cancer. It has always been a life mission of mine to help out a person in need, especially mothers. I think my interest in prioritizing mothers resonates with me. Being a mother who has been victimized by breast cancer gives me a sense of empathy towards all of the other mothers fighting the same battle. It was my worst nightmare to think of a world where my young boys would grow up losing their mother too soon. No child should lose their mother to this horrible disease, and I want to do my part in helping families just like my own.

Being able to contribute to the comfort in at least one person's treatment will be a success for me. I began writing about this part of my life just to share my experience. Possibly being the reason for choosing the path they take with their experience or even instilling a little hope. The most important factor that drove me to write this book and share my life experiences with you is to heighten the level of change I strive to make. I aim to create a foundation that will help donate proceeds from this book to individuals who are battling breast cancer. Although the goal was and still is for my book to give those who are reading, insight about into my experience, it is more than that for me. My motive is to make the lasting difference I had always wanted to make.

Chapter Ten

MALIBU II

I'm in Malibu. A place dreamed of by people worldwide, and a dream that is too farfetched for people in my hometown. A place where freedom is embedded in the reality of those who find themselves there. Feeling the breeze of the cool, clean air in Malibu is itself enough to make you fall in love with the city. Breathing in fresh air isn't so readily available to the people of Iran today. Over the years, Iran has become increasingly polluted. I was lucky enough to grow up in Iran during a time where fresh air was normal and not seen as a luxury.

The ocean usually represents freedom, but what I experienced in Iran as a teenager was anything but free. For women in Iran, even the sight of an ocean was the furthest thing from freedom. This is because that for over forty years now, women have had to abide by the modesty laws enforced in Iran even in a place as unrestricted as the beach. Women are required to remain fully clothed while they watch the men and children enjoy the waves. Although women are not able to expose their bodies, they are still allowed to have access to the ocean fully clothed. As you can imagine, entering the water with your clothes on isn't a very appealing thought.

For Iranian women, the sea's meaning is different from that of the rest of the world because it reminds them of their limitations for even life's simplest wonders, such as going in the ocean. I feel fortunate for the chance of experiencing the peace of swimming in the Caspian Sea, and feeling the water on the few open areas of my body, face, hands, and feet.

But despite the incredible serenity I felt being at the beach in Iran, there was still something missing. The thought of putting my feet in the water without the consequences of being charged with a misdemeanor or other cruel punishment is nothing short of liberating; a feeling I did not experience until I found myself standing on the sands of California.

Yes, now I am in Malibu. It is the dreamland of California in the United States where the air blows through my single ponytail as I walk through the city in just a hairband, shorts, and a T-shirt. In other words, wearing whatever I want in a place that I now finally consider a place of freedom. The sensation of the air and the wind upon my fresh bare skin is priceless; a very simple human pleasure—one which my fellow Iranian women are prohibited from enjoying. I have closed my eyes countless times on the sand, which is now my backyard, trying to take in the wonderful ocean breeze and savor how blessed I am to be on this side of the world. The side where the ocean no longer represents limitation, but instead freedom.

I always look back and think about everything I went through to get here. I think about how many doors remained closed and obstructions that were thrown my way. Then I think about my birthplace and reminisce about old times. I was only a teenager when I developed a love for swimming, which began at the beach of The Caspian Sea. Its saltwater would burn my eyes and mouth, especially on hot summer days, but swimming there was still my favorite. The Caspian Sea is a landlocked sea between Asia and Europe. It is the world's largest inland body of water and has characteristics common to both seas and lakes. I swam in the Caspian Sea water many times when I was a child, like children in the United States.

After the revolution, women were not exempt from their dress codes even at the beach. Long tunics were required for going in the water, so I would still love to go in, but the heavy garments really weighed me down. Women in Iran must always wear a long tunic over their regular clothes and cover their heads with a scarf. It is a law to respect the Islamic rules. A dress code that applied to swimming in public beaches in Iran made it difficult for swimming, but the love of swimming in the ocean was something that always excited me. I end every trip down memory lane with the thought of my success at overcoming everything that could have prevented me from living the life I do today. Now when I look at the ocean, I don't just see it as a place of newfound freedom, but as a place of resilience.

How daring of me to dream about a modern lifestyle, exercising gender equality all while growing up in an Islamic country! I wanted to be free. I wanted to dress as I wished and, most importantly, enjoy life in the way that I wanted. I remember being a member of the Armenian club as my after school extracurricular activity. I would usually take a taxi or sometimes a bus (which I hated taking) to our club meetings. I was also in the theater production, where I would take classes on stage performing arts. I loved being on stage and even pictured myself as another person when I would play the roles of different characters. Role-playing allowed me to step into a different reality other than my own, and I would really get to know the character I was playing. This would make me feel the same form of escape from reality in the same way my book characters would.

The few roles that I was cast for in the plays were minimal, but the very last part I got was in a comedy. It was more of a skit, but I played the role as the leading actress. I went home one night after auditioning with a bunch of other club members, and we got stopped by some pasdars (the Islamic Revolutionary armed forces). I knew how easily my life would change if they decided to take me in. The pasdars were founded in 1979 after the

Islamic Revolution and were the official police force in Iran. Some friends and I were driving home after a successful play rehearsal with my face covered in heavy stage makeup. I was well aware of the punishments that followed breaking the laws set by the Islamic Republic. Legal penalties for things like disobeying the dress code included a prison sentence or even torture. When the pasdars walked up to my friends and me, the first thing I did was close my eyes and pray.

I prayed and prayed, thinking about all of the things that could happen to us for having makeup on. We were detained for two hours, and we never found out what they were doing for two hours. We tried to explain the situation and told them that we were on our way home from an Armenian club where we were rehearsing. My hijab was not fully covering my head. Don't forget the stage makeup, and above all that, there were men, not related to me, in the car. With Iran under Islamic rule, girls were never allowed to socialize with boys in public unless they were somehow related to you. Stuck in our misfortune, we were three girls and two boys in the same car. The only thing I asked myself was, "Will I get arrested? Will I go to jail for that and be punished for my actions? Will I get whipped?"

For being involved in actions that are so ordinary in Western culture that they go unnoticed, my life, wellbeing, and future was at stake. Two hours felt like a lifetime. Thank you, God, for answering my prayers that night. The pasdars let us walk away punishment free. Who did they contact that took two hours, and why did they let us go. Answering these questions was the least of our concerns. Our freedom was given back to us, and that's all that mattered. I can still remember the pasdar's face sneering at me and saying, "...maybe next time you won't be so lucky! Maybe you should accept that you are living in a Muslim country, and if you're not happy, then you can leave!" I listened quietly. But what I really wanted to do was scream back and tell him I did want to leave, but there was always something stopping me.

The difficulty of getting the opportunity to leave Iran with the intention of eventually living in America was standing in our way. When the pasdars stopped my theater friends and me, never would I have thought I would call a place like Malibu home. Feeling helpless in that time of fear was blurring the sight of the possibility of obtaining freedom. The freedom which I am gifted every day in Malibu could have never been imagined at that time. This is normal however, not being able to imagine yourself and the exact components of your life in the future. Looking back to that time in my life, I would feel hopeless, but always optimistic that I would one day live in a free land.

One specific day during our search for freedom, my family and I had our passports ready, patiently waiting for our interview with the American Embassy. My brother was in the U.S. studying engineering when we finally decided to act on our hopes of moving to America. We were trying to get our process of immigration going when life was playing games on us. It is as if things were falling apart just to make the process for us harder. We were waiting for our interviews when we heard that the American Embassy had been taken over by Islamic followers as well as our passports and all of the essential papers regarding our immigration. Moving to America had come to a halt once again.

It was November 4, 1979 when a group of Iranian college students belonging to the Muslim Student Followers of the Imam's Line, who supported the Iranian revolution, took over the U.S. Embassy in Tehran. For one year, two months, and two weeks, from Nov. 4, 1979 to January 20, 1981, fifty-two American diplomats and citizens were held, hostage. Just about ten months after the Iranian revolution, the Islamic Revolution began on February 11, 1979, after Ayatollah Khomeini returned to Iran on February 1, 1979, after 15 years of exile. The Shah and his family had fled the country two weeks before that incident, and Iranian revolutionaries were eager to establish a fundamentalist Islamic government under Khomeini's leadership.

Once again, my family's and my dream to move to the U.S. had to be put on hold for an unknown period. We had no passports, and no documents. They were all taken with the Embassy. I was living my life day to day and getting used to the country's situation but still looking into finding a way to get out of Iran and remained hopeful of doing so.

Meanwhile, I was in my teen years and like any other

Armenian teenage girl, I loved to go to the Armenian stadium and cheer for the athletes. Besides my love for basketball, I was interested in gymnastics and dance, but I loved watching all of the games in our Armenian recreation center. The whole experience was nothing short of memorable. Sitting with my friends and cheering on our local girls and boys as they play their hearts out in either soccer or basketball was one of my favorite past times. Every year in September, a few weeks before the start of the school year, we had the Armenian Olympics which consisted of all kinds of sports. They were held at the Armenian stadium, Ararat Stadium every September 22nd.

September 22nd was always a special day because of this tradition, but this date soon signified another unforgettable event. I was so excited about the Armenian Olympics closing game. It was something I looked forward to all year. My friends and I were sitting in the arena, and suddenly, a loud bang -like an explosion- shook me to my heart's core. My heart was pounding, and I was terrified like never before as I watched people running and screaming to escape the stadium. What is happening? What is going on this time? Are we going to get out of there alive? Who is attacking whom? We were unclear about how this happened. I was unaware that there was an ongoing border dispute and political turmoil between Iran and Iraq. Iraq had invaded Iran.

As a teenage girl, I wasn't paying much attention to politics. I was busy with school, my acting classes, gymnastics, and dancing. The Armenian club of which I was a member, kept me very busy, and I had no time to follow the country's messy political affairs. Besides my books, I drowned myself in music, which slowly turned into my best friend. Music really helped fill all of the gaps in my life. I listened to music when I was lonely, when I was sad, and when I was happy and wanted to dance. Music became a part of me and was present through all of my emotions I felt whether it was good or bad. Living in my small world and trying to fit in, I was always confused about what was happening to my country or my actual surroundings. For just a young little girl, I had seen more than some adults had their entire lifetime. I learned not to trust anything or anybody, but only what and who I knew. Even when I tried my hardest to stay strong, life did not fail to one-up me. My father's unfortunate betrayal, his mysterious death, the Revolution, the hostage-taking of the American Embassy, and now, war.

The Iran-Iraq War was a war between Iraq and Iran's armed forces, which lasted from September 1980 to August 1988. The war began when Iraq invaded Iran on September 22, 1980, the day of the Armenian games. After a long history of border disputes and demands to overthrow Saddam Hussein's regime. Iraqi forces did well at the beginning of the war, taking Iranian Khuzestan, but not too long after, they were stopped and forced out of Iran. The war continued for years, and neither side gained much ground. About a million soldiers and civilians perished. Despite several calls to end the fighting by the United Nations Security Council, the two countries fought until August 20,1988. The Iran-Iraq war was also significant because of Iraq's use of chemical and biological warfare against Iranian troops and civilians.

Living in Iran for four years during the war with fear and uncertainty was far worse than the war itself. During these four long years, there were countless nights that turned from fun youthful gatherings into hiding for safety. When the emergency sirens would ring throughout our city, my loved ones and I would gather under the staircase waiting for the all-clear sign. Usually, my mom, my two sisters, and, I waited for hours under that staircase, sometimes until morning. The bombardments happened at night, and we would hear the outcome of what destruction occurred the next morning. It was one of the most terrifying things I have ever experienced in my childhood years.

There is always the calm after the storm. My calm comes in waves, but it did come. I experienced many stormy days in my childhood and saw things that an average child would never have seen in their life: death, war, and hardship. I endured the stormiest days with the most thunder, but I also experienced many beautiful, irreplaceable memories. There is always sunlight between storms, and my friends, family, and hobbies I cherished were my sunlight. In the way my story was written, through all of the difficult moments filled with sadness and the happy one, it was my own unique original copy, and I wouldn't want it written any other way.

Yes, I am in Malibu. The warm sunny breeze is blowing through my hair as I am standing on the balcony of our beach house overlooking the waves, thinking about how drastically life can change. I reminisce about my past, but I was always a fan of looking forward while appreciating the present. When I am in Malibu, I not only enjoy being there, but I reminisce on my journey prior to ending up where I am today. Being on the beach makes me realize how life can change so quickly and drastically. As humans, we can experience the highest tides, and the lowest, which is how life is meant to be. I remember how different the meaning of the beach was to me many years ago compared to what it means to me today. Our lives are constantly changing whether we like it or not, and this is how mine did.

Acknowledgments

I want to thank Frank Eastland and Bob Laning from Publish Authority for their indispensable hard work in bringing life to my story and treating it with the same regard as if it were their own.

I also want to thank my niece, Bronte A. Yarkhoda for assisting me in editing my story in a way which captures my vision so authentically.

About the Author

Violet Baghdasarian is an Armenian American and author of her autobiography *Tehran to Malibu*. Born in Iran, she has lived all over the world in a life plentiful of influences, relocating to Germany and making her final transition to her home in America. Various jobs in different career fields have successfully supported her independent lifestyle. She lives every day by incorporating her unique twist to "everything happens for a reason." She resides in Malibu, California, with her loving family.

For more about the author, she invites you to visit her website at TehranToMalibu.com.

Thank You for Reading

Publish Authority

If you enjoyed *Tehran to Malibu,* we invite you to share your thoughts and reactions online and with friends and family.

www.ingramcontent.com/pod-product-compliance
Lightning Source LLC
Chambersburg PA
CBHW071419070526
44578CB00003B/611